T3-BID-979

JUVENILE VANDALISM

JUVENILE VANDALISM

A STUDY OF ITS NATURE AND PREVENTION

By

JOHN M. MARTIN
Assistant Professor of Sociology
Fordham University
New York City

CHARLES C THOMAS • PUBLISHER
Springfield • Illinois • U.S.A.

CHARLES C THOMAS • PUBLISHER
BANNERSTONE HOUSE
301-327 East Lawrence Avenue, Springfield, Illinois, U.S.A.

Library of Congress Catalog Card Number: 60-14750

With THOMAS BOOKS careful attention is given to all details of manufacturing and design. It is the Publisher's desire to present books that are satisfactory as to their physical qualities and artistic possibilities and appropriate for their particular use. THOMAS BOOKS will be true to those laws of quality that assure a good name and good will.

Printed in the United States of America

To My Parents

PREFACE

MUCH has been written about juvenile delinquency, but comparatively little has been written about vandalism as a type of delinquency. This is a book about vandalism.

I first became interested in the topic several years ago while teaching at another university. After class one day a student asked me to tell her what I could about the subject. What prompted her inquiry has long been forgotten, but I have not forgotten the reply I was forced to give her. After thinking about it for a while, I realized I knew practically nothing about vandalism, and I told her so.

Shortly after this I began combing the literature for information about vandalism. My search was generally unrewarding. Little attention had been given to vandalism by students of delinquency. References to the topic were conspicuously absent from the usual textbooks in criminology and juvenile delinquency, although occasionally incidents of vandalism were briefly described in the standard monographs on delinquency. The bulk of the material I uncovered, however, was contained in articles and editorials in various periodicals and magazines, most of which had been written since 1940, although a few dated as far back as 1909-1916. In spite of their number, most of these references contained little real information about vandals or vandalism. Usually their authors simply pointed up the seriousness of the problem. Sometimes they offered "explanations" of such behavior, but almost always without supporting data. Frequently these references concluded by urging that "measures" be taken to curb vandalism.

Convinced that vandalism would make a good topic for research, I decided that when the opportunity arose I would do a study of vandalism. The chapters that follow describe the study I was able to carry out.

It is impractical to try to enumerate all those who, through their co-operation, criticism, and suggestion, have assisted me in writing this book. I must, however, acknowledge my indebtedness to John Warren Hill, former Presiding Justice of the New York Domestic Relations Court, to Marion M. Brennan of the probation staff in the same Court, to Ralph W. Whalen, Commissioner of Youth Services for New York City, to Maude M. Craig of the New York City Youth Board, and to the late William A. Hamm, Associate Superintendent of the New York City Board of Education.

A special note of appreciation is also due to my former teachers at New York University, particularly Frederic M. Thrasher and Dan W. Dodson, to my colleagues at Fordham University, Rev. Joseph P. Fitzpatrick, S.J., and Nicholas S. Timasheff, and to Thomas F. O'Dea of the University of Utah.

I am also indebted to Thelma G. Martin whose encouragement, sound advice, and very practical typing assistance were freely given throughout the project.

Finally I must thank various informants, some of whose case histories are presented in the following pages, for their interest and co-operation in supplying much of the raw data for this study.

Throughout the book the names of vandals, gangs, victims, schools, and other individuals, groups, and organizations have been deleted or changed wherever it was necessary to avoid working undue hardships on the people concerned.

JOHN M. MARTIN

Fordham University

CONTENTS

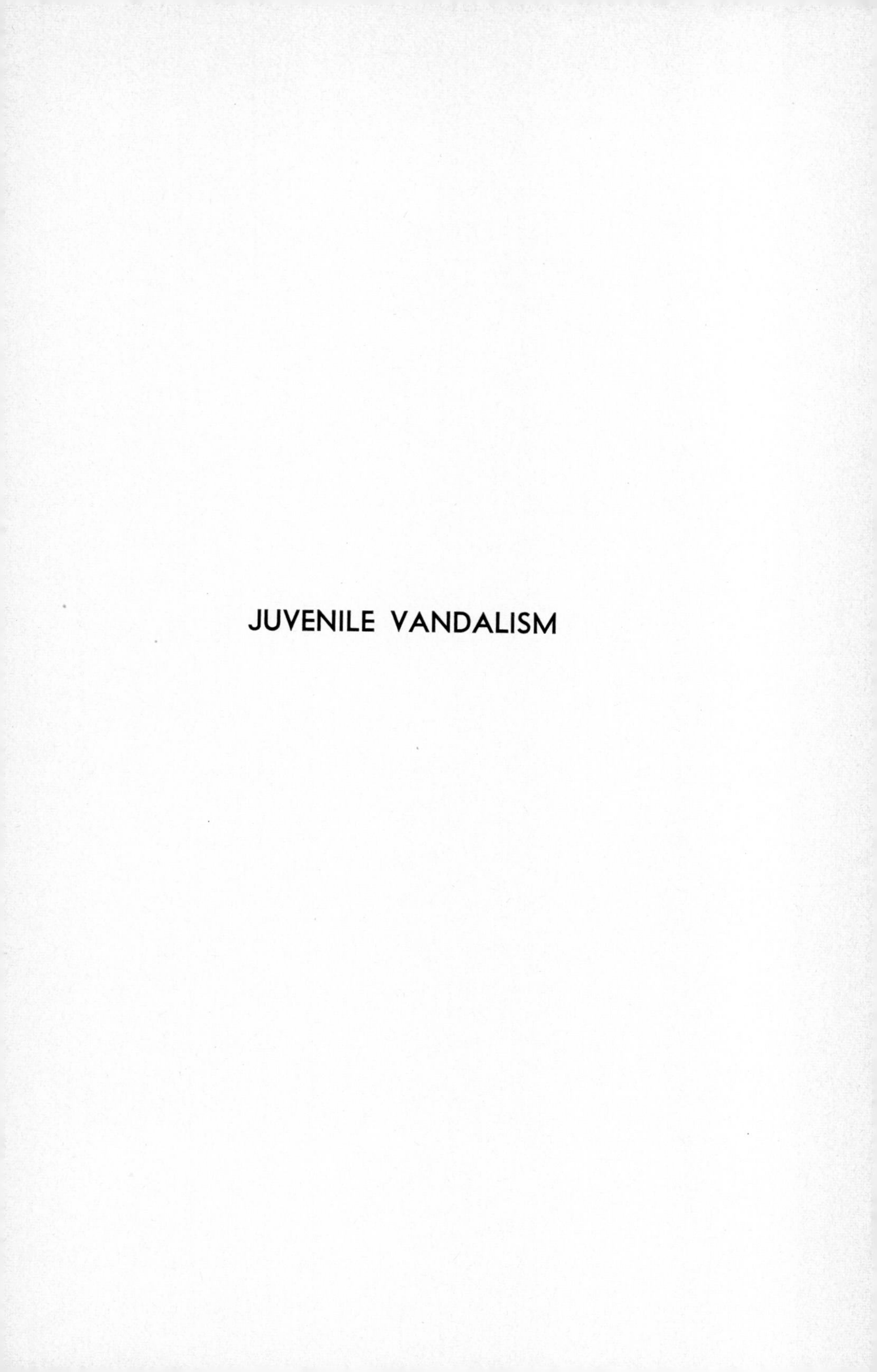

JUVENILE VANDALISM

Vandals on Rampage

30 Dozen Eggs Daub School in Amityville

Special to World-Telegram and Sun.

AMITYVILLE, L. I., Dec. 14.—Amityville Memorial High School was a swamp of smashed eggs and spilt ink today—the target of weekend vandalism.

Police and school officials are still trying to assess the damage, which may run into thousands of dollars.

Entry was through a smashed kitchen door. Inside, 30 dozen eggs had been splattered on the floor, and celery, tomatoes and cheese were smeared everywhere.

The path of devastation led through the shattered glass doors of the infirmary, from which scissors, razor blades and a scalpel disappeared. Six vials of adrenalin also were unaccounted for.

In the offices adjoining, typewriters had been gummed up, papers strewn on the floor and everything blotched with ink.

The office of the principal, Edward Cap, had also been vandalized—debris was ankle-deep and the filing cabinets were swathed in adhesive tape.

Officials recalled a similar incident, costing more than than $1000, in 1953.

Vandals Damage 46 Cars

LOS ANGELES, Nov. 22 (UP)—Forty-six new cars on display at the Los Angeles international auto show were damaged by vandals, operators of the show discovered today. Damage to the autos was estimated at $50,000 by Charles H. Elmendorf, show manager.

VANDALS MAR HOMES

Proposed Biracial Project Near Chicago Damaged

Special to The New York Times.

CHICAGO, Dec. 17—Vandalism was reported today for the first time in the interracial housing dispute in suburban Deerfield.

Max Weinrib, vice president and building supervisor of Progress Development Corporation, reported to the police that nineteen studs in two of the concern's uncompleted houses in the village had been chopped off.

The houses are the first of fifty-one [...] to build [...] enable Ne[...] of the hou[...] by some r[...]

Mr. Wei[...] of the hou[...] at the req[...] ing officia[...] survey, p[...] mine the [...] structures.

Meanwh[...] were urge[...] Church F[...] Chicago [...] the oppor[...] village.

Westchester Board Halts School Buses In Pupil Vandalism

Special to The New York Times.

ARMONK VILLAGE, N. Y., Feb. 5—School bus service between this northern Westchester community and Pleasantville High School was halted "indefinitely" this morning because student vandals failed to respond to a school board ultimatum.

On Monday and again on Wednesday unidentifed students slashed cushion seats on a bus that carries pupils home late in the afternoon at the close of athletic and club activities at the school. These incidents, school officials said, followed a pattern of rowdiness and vandalism covering a period of several years.

Yesterday, Charles E. Pound, president of the board of Union Free School District 5, warned that bus service would be suspended unless the guilty students surrendered or were "turned in."

[...] of Armonk's seventy-[...]ondary school pupils [...] the five miles to school [...]ly organized car pools [...]driven by their parents. [...]ailed to show up at all, [...]g to Police Chief John [...]enhan.

[...] parents there was talk [...] appealing to the State [...]ent of Education to [...] restoration of service. [...]ggested that it might [...]ssary to seek a court [...]recting the state agency

[...]ound reported late to-[...] the vandals had failed [...]fy themselves and that [...] but "informed," fellow [...] had proved unwilling [...] the culprits or put [...] upon them to confess.

Held in $5,000 For Vandalism At Synagogue

By WILLIAM NEUGEBAUER

A 22-year-old gas station attendant, free in $1,500 bail pending sentencing on a felonious assault charge, was grabbed in Brooklyn yesterday while, police said, he was damaging a synagogue in a drunken rage.

Vandals Wreck Blind Man's Boat

WARREN, R. I., Oct. 13 (AP)—A blind Pawtucket man who reconditioned a 2[...] boat for himself la[...] terday found it wr[...] dals at its summer [...] Kickemuit river h[...]

Walter Moore, 33 [...] dale avenue, told [...] that 33 holes had [...] and hacked in the [...] sides, the windshi[...] dows and rudder [...] the anchor, propel[...] shaft and running [...]

He discovered t[...] when he came here [...] boat home for the winter.

Blame Students For Vandalism In Lynn School

Schoolboys are believed responsible for a carnival of vandalism during the weekend at the Cobbett Junior High School in Lynn.

Damage to two safes in the building indicated that robbery may have been the original motive.

Temple Emanu-El Wall Defaced With Swastika

A swastika two and a half feet square was painted in black last night on an outside wall of the community house [o]f Temple Emanu-[...] Sixty-fifth Street. [...]um is around the [...] the temple, which [...] Avenue.

[...]tika was discov-[...] P. M. by Patrol-[...]m Purcell. The [...]still wet, and the [...]ed it off the wall [...]tine.

[...]ve been no other [...] incidents in the [...]d recently, the

Vandals Topple 187 Gravestones

MELROSE, Nov. 16 (AP)—Police today sought a group of vandals who went on a rampage in Wyoming cemetery and toppled 187 headstones.

Thirty headstones were smashed in the desecration which Police Capt. George MacWilliams called the aftermath of a wild party last night.

MacWilliams said 10 to 12 persons must have spent several hours in the cemetery to cause the destruction.

William J. McClintock, chairman of the City Cemetery committee, estimated damages at $7000.

Subway Ride Was Smashing

Two young couples who allegedly smashed 15 subway light bulbs, in what their court-appointed lawyer called "the spirit of the moment," were held in $1,000 bail each on malicious mischief charges yesterday in Weekend Court.

Ipswich Youths Ordered to Pay For Vandalism

IPSWICH—Two Ipswich youths Thursday were placed on two years' probation and ordered to pay for damage in excess of $2000 which they caused the Ipswich Public Library.

HELD IN LEVITTOWN BIAS

Man Said to Admit Painting 'KKK' Near Negro's Home

LEVITTOWN, Pa., Oct. 18 (AP)—A Levittown man was under $500 bail today charged with painting "KKK" on a wall near the home of Levittown's first Negro family. The initials are those of the Ku Klux Klan, long an anti-Negro organization.

Vandals Mar Reunion of Iron Curtain Family

CHICAGO (UPI) — Vandals marred the happy reunion yesterday of a family separated for 16 years by the Iron Curtain.

They smeared the back windows of Paulius Leonas' home with oil as the Lithuanian family slept after an hours-long party celebrating the "homecoming" of his children—Regina, 20, and Tomas, 18.

The vandals also smashed the front window of Leonas' real estate office, and reports to police kept the joyous father too busy to breakfast with his children on their first morning in the United States.

The brother and sister, permitted to come to America after Soviet Premier Nikita Khrushchev kept a promise to their parents, arrived in Chicago Thursday for a tumultous reception at Midway Airport and a big celebration at their parents' home.

"I don't mind the windows because I have insurance," Leonas said. "But it upsets me that people should do such a thing on a day like this."

Thursday the beaming father had exclaimed, "there has not been such a day since the world was created. Our hearts cannot hold the joy of this event."

Vandals Raid Brooklyn School And Synagogue

Vandals broke into the Rabbi Chaim Berlin Yeshiva, 1899 Prospect Place, in the Brownsville section of Brooklyn, early yesterday. Entering a first floor synagogue, they ripped up a sacred scroll, shredded prayer books, smashed ceremonial objects, chairs and benches, and defaced walls.

On the second floor of the three-story building, they invaded classrooms and tore up books, broke chairs and desks, tossed inkwells around and [...] containing [...] charity. [...]diate esti-[...]

[...] building's [...]nez, forty, [...]ent apart-[...] heard a [...] a. m. but [...]because he [...]ning."

[...]noy, prin-[...] about 400 [...]ary school [...]n the syn-[...]

[...]e of the [...]marked, in [...], with let-[...]the name [...]robably a misspelling of "Roman Lords," a neighborhood youth gang on which rivals possibly were trying to pin the blame for the vandalism.

The damage was discovered at 7 a. m. Twelve detectives were assigned to investigate.

Miami Blackout Tied to 3 Teens

By the Associated Press.

MIAMI, Feb. 22.—Three teenagers were arrested and charged with causing t[...] struction which knocke[...] electric power all alon[...] southeast Florida Gold [...]

The boys were arrest[...] last thursday night. [...] classrooms yesterday at [...] Jackson High School.

Sgt. Pat Gallagher o[...] sheriff's department sai[...] boys admitted firing abou[...] rounds of ammunition [...] high voltage lines of the [...]t Co. [...] pl[...] Mia[...] into [...] fo[...]s in [...] the youths admitting they had for three [...]

[...]f of the [...]reau of in-[...]e youths [...]tids. They [...] trouble be-[...] the youths [...]ent. [...] malicious [...]e property [...]he youths [...]sed under

Painting of Ike Slashed in Club

By the Associated Press.

HOUSTON, March 10.—A portrait of President Eisenhower, hung in the exclusive Houston Club, was found slashed last night. A note tacked to the frame said: "We don't like Ike in Texas."

The oil painting by Boris B. Gordon was about a year old. It had been in the club 10 days and was valued at $1000. Club manager Henry O. Barbour said the painting was to be sent to the Texas Capitol in Austin. Police had no suspects.

Vandals Smash Altar In Chicago Church

United Press International.

CHICAGO, Dec. 21.—Vandals broke into one of Chicago's oldest churches today and used sledge hammers to smash a marble altar said to have been worth at least $10,000 when first built.

Police said the vand[...] parently took advantage [...] noise of a passing e[...] train to break in by sm[...] a panel in a rear door [...] James Catholic Church.

Father John Farrell [...] vandals then com[...] smashed a side altar, [...] as the St. James altar, [...] 84-year-old church. He s[...] vandals also broke into [...] but were unable to [...] valuable chalices and other ceremonial vessels through a hole in the side.

School Vandalism Increases Yearly

By JANE NELSON

Cost of replacing windows broken at city schools by vandals has been increasing $1,000 a year since 1950, Horace E. Boggy said today.

The buildings and grounds manager said 3,663 windows were smashed in city school buildings last school year (1956-57). Replacement costs totaled $18,344.

[...] 90% of it is [...]aid.

[...] average of [...]ases) a week. [...] start fires." [...] high schools [...] broken last [...]t that was [...] 22 at 1231 S. [...] 157 were [...] [...]on and Manual High Schools reported 86 broken windows each last school year; Broad Ripple 75, Tech 73, Wood 48, Shortridge 46 and Howe 29.

A fire started with paper in a classroom at School 41, 3002 Rader, last year caused $1,200 damage, Boggy said.

Boggy said the main purpose of the break-ins appeared to be the theft of money. Acts of vandalism then often accompany the break-in, he added.

Last Saturday at School 90, 3351 W. 18th, custodian Allen M. Nelson reported a cafeteria door broken and eggs and oranges thrown about the premises. Ink also was splat[tered] about the building, incl[uding] the auditorium. A soft [...] machine was broken and typewriters and an a[...] machine stolen.

119 WINDOWS IN ONE SCHOOL

Among the other [...] schools where a large [...] ber of windows were br[...] last school year, Boggy [re]ported, were School 47, [...] W. Ray, 119; School 24, [...] W. North, 116, and Schoo[l ...] 1002 W. 25th, 110.

Boggy said "it is impos[sible] to determine the total pri[ce] what vandalism costs [...] schools each year." He p[oint]ed out that some equip[ment] stolen is later recovered.

Boggy said night watch[men] are employed at all city schools, a precaution w[hich] he said undoubtedly cuts [van]dalism.

Swastikas Found On Jersey Graves

Special to World-Telegram and Sun.

EAST BRUNSWICK, N. J., March 11.—The black swastika, symbol of Hitler's Third Reich, was discovered early today painted on 158 gravestones in Beth Abraham Cemetery, Cranbury-South River Rd.

SWASTIKA INCIDENT AIMED AT ADENAUER

Special to The New York Times.

WASHINGTON, March 17—A minor incident marred Chancellor Adenauer's final day in Washington.

When he visited the National Gallery of Art, he signed the guest book. Someone in the crowd then scrawled two swastikas, the symbols of nazism, on the book.

Secretary of State Christian A. Herter issued the following statement on the incident:

"I was shocked to hear of the deplorable incident which occurred at the National Gallery of Art this morning when someone scribbled swastikas at the top of the page on which Chancellor Adenauer signed the gallery guest book. This vicious and inexcusable act is a reflection not upon the Chancellor, against whom it was directed, but upon the warped individual who was responsible for it. This act of vandalism is all the more despicable in view of the Chancellor's record of active opposition to, and condemnation of, the Nazi movement and his distinguished leadership of post-war Germany along the paths of freedom and democracy."

Vandals Slash L.I. Car Tires

Special to World-Telegram and Sun.

BALDWIN, L. I., Feb. 12.—Vandals armed with knives and ice picks slashed 45 tires on 20 cars here during the night. Nassau County police awakened the owners of the disabled vehicles before dawn this morning so they wouldn't be late for work.

NEGROES' HOME STONED

Whites Protest in 2 Incidents Near Wilmington, Del.

WILMINGTON, Del., Feb. 24 (AP)—A Negro family moved into the all-white suburb of Collins Park today, touching off two outbreaks. In one the Negroes' home was stoned.

Chapter I

INTRODUCTION

THE newspaper headlines on the opposing page and the following photographs illustrate vandalism as it occurs in American communities.

The exact cost of vandalism is incalculable. Certainly property losses from such destruction total millions of dollars annually. But the financial cost of vandalism is only a partial measure of its seriousness as a social problem. In its various forms vandalism also threatens some of our society's most cherished non-pecuniary values, including those of racial and religious tolerance, the non-violent and rational settlement of conflict, and the conviction that property, quite aside from its real worth, should not be wantonly abused or destroyed.

Despite the loss from vandalism and the special efforts to prevent its occurrence in various communities, surprisingly little attention has been given to this form of delinquency by sociologists, psychiatrists, and other students of juvenile misconduct. Several years ago an article published in *Federal Probation* as part of a "Symposium on Vandalism" noted that, although it was possible to build up a substantial library about such subjects as arson, assault, burglary, kleptomania, runaways, sex misconduct, and truancy, the voluminous professional literature on juvenile delinquency was virtually silent on vandalism. The article further suggested that vandalism, as a type of delinquency, occurs as frequently in every-day life as do other types of misbehavior. For these reasons, the article proposed that vandalism should become a priority subject for research.[1]

---

[1] D. H. MacNeil: Is vandalism actually on the increase? *Federal Probation,* 18 (March, 1954), p. 16.

More recently, noting the magnitude of the problem of vandalism, the scarcity of professional literature on the subject, and the need for research to guide programs aimed at reducing juvenile delinquency, the United States Senate Subcommittee to Investigate Juvenile Delinquency also proposed that vandalism should become a priority topic for study.[2]

DEFINITION OF VANDALISM

The noun "vandalism" was reputedly coined in 1794 by an apologist for the French Revolution who, attempting to cast blame for the destruction of works of art during the Revolution upon its enemies, likened such destruction to the behavior of the Vandals, an East Germanic tribe, who sacked Rome in the Fifth Century.[3]

Although the word "vandalism" is still used occasionally to describe the willful or ignorant destruction of artistic or literary treasures, and sometimes refers to such behaviors as littering and out-of-season hunting, it is most commonly used today to describe the destruction of property in general, especially by children and youths.[4] In fact a recent effort to define more precisely the content of such behavior suggested that vandalism meant "the deliberate defacement, mutilation or destruction of private or public property by a juvenile or group of juveniles not having immediate or direct ownership in the property so abused."[5]

In the present study vandalism was defined as the offense "malicious mischief," specifically the willful destruction, damage, or defacement of property. This usage is in keeping with the

---

[2] United States Congress, Senate Committee on the Judiciary, *Juvenile Delinquency*, Report of Subcommittee, 85th Congress, 1st Session, on S. Res. 173, 84th Congress, 2d Session. Washington, Government Printing Office, 1957, pp. 127-132.

[3] S. J. Idzerda: Iconoclasm during the French Revolution. *American Historical Review*, 60 (October, 1954), pp. 13-26.

[4] See, e.g., E. C. Waggener: Remedies for vandalism. *Nation's Schools*, 26 (September, 1940), p. 58; Vandalism. *Recreation*, 43 (July, 1949), p. 214; Halloween and hooliganism. *Senior Scholastic*, 67 (October 27, 1955), pp. 7-8; M. M. Eliot: What is vandalism? *Federal Probation*, *op. cit.*, pp. 3-5.

[5] M. B. Clinard and A. L. Wade: Toward the delineation of vandalism as a subtype in juvenile delinquency. *The Journal of Criminal Law, Criminology and Police Science*, 48 (January-February, 1958), pp. 493-499.

definition of vandalism as general property destruction offered in the *Corpus Juris Secundum*.[6] It is also in accord with the conclusion of insurance underwriters who, finding vandalism *per se* unknown as a distinct offense in the law, suggested that property loss from vandalism is covered by policies protecting against "malicious mischief," which is defined generally as the willful or wanton and malicious destruction, damage, or defacement of property.[7]

ORIENTATION TO PRESENT STUDY

Delinquency consists of many kinds of deviant behavior committed by different types of juvenile offenders for various purposes in a variety of concrete situations. Juvenile auto thieves, rapists, and truants are not all cast from the same mold. Auto theft, rape, and truancy are not replicas one of another. These offenses are not usually committed to achieve the same ends or purposes; nor do they occur in the same kinds of situations. Therefore, we must not be concerned with general explanations of delinquency as if, like measles, it were "a homogeneous something that people either have or have not and that it is sufficient, therefore, simply to note that a person either is or is not a 'delinquent.' "[8] We must, instead, isolate and study particular types of delinquency, describe the characteristics of the individuals involved in each type, and determine, as best we can, the purposes of their behavior and the kinds of situations in which it occurs. Once determined these variations may be used as guideposts in the selection of programs especially suited to preventing the particular type of delinquency isolated.

Medical researchers and practitioners no longer attempt to study, treat, and prevent disease in general. They isolate malaria, tuberculosis, poliomyelitis and other kinds of diseases and deal

---

[6] *Corpus Juris Secundum.* Brooklyn, New York, American Law Book Company, 1955, p. 802.

[7] *Digest of Statutes and Notation of Cases Respecting Riot, Malicious Mischief and Vandalism in States in Western Underwriters Association Territory.* Chicago, Western Underwriters Association, 1949, pp. 4-5.

[8] A. K. Cohen: *Delinquent Boys: The Culture of the Gang.* Glencoe, Illinois, The Free Press, 1955, p. 172.

separately with each. This practice makes good sense in medicine; it also makes good sense in the field of delinquency.

The present research is an exploratory study of vandalism as a subtype in delinquency. Most of the data were obtained from an examination of apprehended juvenile vandals and the vandalism they committed in the Borough of The Bronx, New York City,[9] in 1955. Additional data were derived from newspaper reports about incidents of vandalism, from descriptions of vandalism in the literature, and from various other sources.

Basic to the study was the assumption that to understand the "whys" of vandalism it was necessary to consider the characteristics of juveniles who commit such delinquency, the quality of their home life and peer group relationships, the neighborhood milieu in which they live and to which they respond, the "objective" aspects of the situations in which vandalism occurs, and the "subjective" definitions of such situations held by vandals themselves. In addition, to achieve a more complete understanding of vandalism it seemed necessary to look beyond the neighborhood milieu in which vandals operate and explore the root characteristics of American society which appear to foster vandalism and other types of crime and delinquency.

Because of the exploratory approach used in this study the conclusions presented in the chapters that follow are offered for the contributions they may make toward a better understanding of vandalism and for the value they may have in developing programs aimed at preventing such property destruction. They are not meant to be construed, however, as final statements regarding the "causes" of vandalism or its prevention. Fundamentally they must be regarded as tentative conceptualizations and hypotheses in need of further testing and verification.

---

[9] The New York City Department of City Planning estimated that in December, 1954, New York City had a total population of 8,050,000: 6,725,000 (83.0%) white, 840,000 (10.4%) non-white, and 485,000 (6.0%) Puerto Rican. Of this total 1,500,000 were estimated to live in the Bronx: 1,255,000 (83.7%) white, 115,000 (7.7%) non-white, and 130,000 (8.6%) Puerto Rican. *Juvenile Delinquency Profile: 1955, New York City.* New York, New York City Youth Board, September, 1956, Table 10, p. 11.

ILLUSTRATIONS OF VANDALISM

(United Press International Photo)

SYNAGOGUE DEFACED BY VANDALS IN HARRISBURG, PENNSYLVANIA

(United Press International Photo)

MONUMENTS AND HEADSTONES TOPPLED OVER BY VANDALS IN ST. LOUIS CEMETERY

(United Press International Photo)

MINER'S HOME DAMAGED BY JUVENILES DURING COPPER COMPANY STRIKE IN BUTTE, MONTANA

TRAFFIC SIGN VANDALISM IN NEW YORK CITY

Vandalism to California state highway signs cost $60,000 in 1947. In the state of Washington, such damage cost more than $43,000 in 1949. (H. D. Clark: Vandalism, our chosen American sport. *Survey*, February, 1950.)

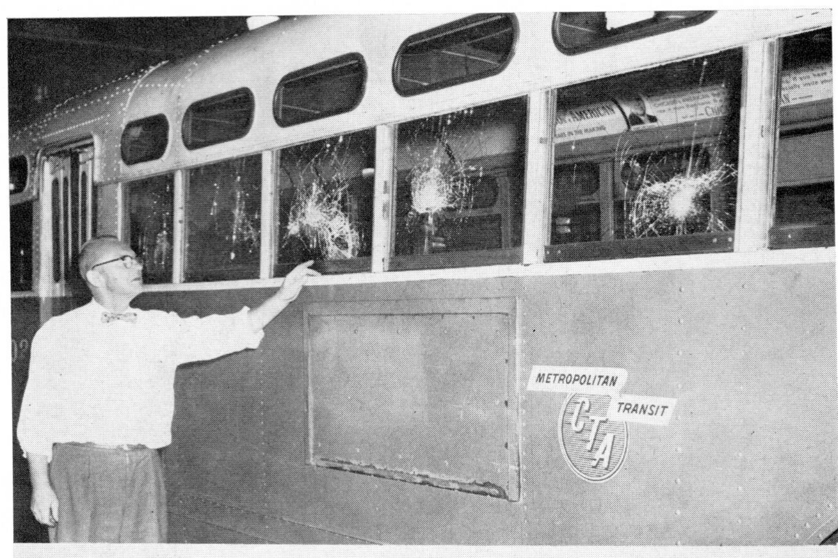

(United Press International Photos)

CHICAGO BUS DAMAGED BY TEENAGERS

During 1950, some nineteen transit companies paid more than $113,000 to repair damage caused by vandals. (F. Otwell: What price vandalism? *Bus Transportation,* March, 1951.)

(Photo Courtesy New York Central System)

RAILROAD COMMUTER CAR OF THE NEW YORK CENTRAL SYSTEM STRIPPED OF BRASS AND COPPER PARTS

Vandalism costs some railroads as much as $100,000 to $2,000,000 a year. (H. S. Dewhurst: *The Railroad Police,* Springfield, Illinois. Charles C Thomas, Publisher, 1955.)

(United Press International Photo)

DETROIT SCHOOL WRECKED BY TWO NINE-YEAR-OLD BOYS

In Boston, the cost of school repairs due to vandalism was $53,752 in 1953. (W. C. Kvaraceus: *The Community and the Delinquent.* Yonkers-on-Hudson, New York, World Book Company, 1954.)

During 1959, there were 160,500 panes of glass broken in New York City schools, with an estimated cost for replacement $401,000. (Letter to author from Deputy Superintendent, Bureau of Plant Operation and Maintenance, New York City Board of Education.)

Paint Daubings in New York City

(Photo Courtesy National Park Service)

STATUE IN NATIONAL PARK DEFACED BY VANDALS

During 1949, vandalism in New York City parks and playgrounds cost over $200,000. (R. Moses: Vandals at work. *Bulletin of the National Association of Secondary School Principals,* October, 1950.)

Chapter II

SOME CHARACTERISTICS OF VANDALS

TIME and time again the issue of "non-representativeness" has been raised regarding criminal and delinquent populations known to the police, courts, and correctional agencies. It is argued, for example, that the law-enforcement process works undue hardships on lower-class people and on members of depressed minority groups. For any offenses they commit, members of these groups are more likely to be arrested, to be found guilty, and to be imprisoned than are their more affluent, prestigeful, and in this sense at least, more fortunate counterparts.

The validity of this argument can scarcely be denied. "Official" criminals and delinquents are not necessarily representative of all offenders. Yet, and this point is frequently overlooked by critics who disparage the study of "official" offenders, much can be learned about crime and delinquency from the examination of such offenders. As Paul W. Tappan has argued in defending the study of convicted offenders:

> It is as futile to contend that this group should not be studied on the grounds that it is incomplete or non-representative as it would be to maintain that psychology should terminate its description, analysis, diagnosis, and treatment of deviants who cannot be completely representative as selected. Convicted persons are nearly all criminals . . . . their origins, traits, dynamics of development, and treatment influences can be studied profitably for purposes of description, understanding and control.[1]

---

[1] P. W. Tappan: Who is the criminal? *American Sociological Review*, 12 (February, 1947), pp. 96-102.

"Official" offenders, then, constitute an important group worthy of study for two reasons. When properly selected, they do represent the kinds of law violators coming before the police, courts, and correctional agencies. Therefore, whatever can be learned about such offenders should not only contribute to our general knowledge of crime and delinquency but should also be of particular interest and value to public and private agencies which on a day-to-day basis must deal with and make decisions about known and convicted offenders.

This chapter has a two-fold purpose: (1) to describe the sex, age, ethnic, and socio-economic characteristics of 291 juvenile vandals known to law-enforcement agencies in New York City; (2) to describe several other characteristics of juvenile vandals derived from an examination of 29 vandals actually adjudicated delinquents in the Children's Court of New York City.

SEX, AGE, ETHNIC, AND SOCIO-ECONOMIC CHARACTERISTICS OF VANDALS

Delinquency statistics indicate: far more boys than girls are involved in delinquency; the majority of delinquent children are fourteen years old or more; disproportionately more delinquents are drawn from the families of marginal groups on the American scene, including urban-drifting Negroes and Spanish-speaking people; delinquents are also disproportionately drawn from families of lower socio-economic status.

Are the sex, age, ethnic, and socio-economic characteristics the same for vandals as for other delinquents? After an appraisal of available information on vandalism as a subtype in juvenile delinquency, Clinard and Wade concluded, on the basis of Children's Bureau statistics and studies in various localities, that far more boys than girls are also involved in vandalism. However, they found that present evidence is in disagreement as to whether pre-adolescents or adolescents are more typically involved in such destruction. They also found that evidence regarding the social class affiliation of vandals is conflicting and fragmentary. Furthermore, they suggested that, although some vandalism may be related to racial, ethnic, or religious prejudice, it is unlikely that the offense is more typical of certain racial or ethnic groups than others.[2]

The present section of this study compares the sex, age, ethnic, and socio-economic characteristics of vandals with those of other delinquents. The vandal group consisted of those juveniles who, while living in the Bronx, New York City, in 1955, committed acts of vandalism and for this reason were enumerated in the Juvenile Delinquency Index of the New York City Youth Board. The other delinquents, or the non-vandal group, consisted of those Bronx juveniles who in 1955 were enumerated in the same Index for offenses not involving vandalism.

The Juvenile Delinquency Index of the New York City Youth Board contains some 34,907 cards representing individuals, six through twenty years of age, who, while residents of New York City, in 1955, were reported by the Juvenile Aid Bureau or the Bureau of Identification of the New York City Police Department, or by the Children's Court Division of the New York City Domestic Relations Court to have committed acts of delinquency. The 34,907 cards represent an unduplicated count of such juveniles based on their first referral to the Police Department or the Children's Court in 1955. Of the 34,907 cards, 7,112 represent Bronx juveniles reported to the Index.

The information recorded on each card in the Index includes the name (in code), address, sex, age, and ethnic characteristics of each juvenile reported, the offense for which he was reported, and the borough and health area in which he lived at the time of this offense.

Inspection of the 7,112 Bronx cards in the Index for 1955 revealed that 291, or 4.1 per cent, of the total Bronx referrals were reported because they had committed acts of vandalism.

Sex Characteristics

Sex was specified for 290 of the 291 Bronx vandals. Of the 7,112 Bronx delinquents enumerated in the Index in 1955, sex

---

[2] M. B. Clinard and A. L. Wade: Toward the delineation of vandalism as a subtype in juvenile delinquency. *The Journal of Criminal Law, Criminology and Police Science,* 48 (January-February, 1958), pp. 493-499.

was specified for 7,063.[3] Subtracting 290 from 7,063 yielded 6,773 delinquents who were reported to the Index in 1955 for offenses not involving vandalism.

Table I compares the sex distribution of the Bronx vandals with the sex distribution of the Bronx delinquents reported for offenses other than vandalism. It should be noted that, although both groups were composed mostly of boys, at the *.05 level of significance*[4] a higher proportion of the vandals were boys (96.9% to 87.6%).

TABLE I

NUMBERS AND PERCENTAGES OF VANDALS AND OTHER DELINQUENTS, BY SEX, THE BRONX, NEW YORK CITY, 1955

	Vandals 6-20 Years Old		*Other Delinquents 6-20 Years Old*		*Difference*
Sex	*Number*	*Per Cent*	*Number*	*Per Cent*	*Per Cent*
Male	281	96.9	5,930	87.6	9.3
Female	9	3.1	843	12.4	-9.3
TOTAL	290	100.0	6,773	100.0	

$X^2 = 22.90; P < .05$

Source: Juvenile Delinquency Index, New York City Youth Board, 1955.

Thus, while the other delinquents were predominantly boys, the vandals were almost exclusively boys.

Other studies also indicate that vandalism as a subtype in delinquency is almost entirely the behavior of boys. Hermann Mannheim, for example, found that of 6,125 delinquents under twenty-one years of age dealt with by the magistrates' courts in Great Britain in 1952 for malicious damage to property, 96.3 per cent were boys.[5] Similar results were obtained in Denver, Colorado. Of a sample of 122 vandals, ten to sixteen years of age, drawn from the records of the Juvenile Bureau of the Denver

[3] *Juvenile Delinquency Profile: 1955, New York City.* New York, New York City Youth Board, September, 1956, Table 12, p. 13.

[4] Throughout this section of the present study .05 was set as the level of significance. Note, however, that differences between the sex (Table I) and age (Table II) of the vandals and the other delinquents were also significant at the .01 level.

[5] H. Mannheim: The problem of vandalism in Great Britain. *Federal Probation,* 18 (March, 1954), pp. 14-15.

Police Department for the period 1944 to early 1954, 93.4 per cent were boys.[6]

All of these results are in general agreement with the findings of a study of vandalism by male and female college students made by W. H. Clark. Perhaps not too surprisingly Clark concluded, in part, not only that boys are more destructive than girls, but also that boys are "more vigorous, bolder, and less inhibited than girls in their destructive escapades."[7]

Age Characteristics

Age was specified for 287 of the 291 Bronx vandals. Of the 7,112 Bronx delinquents enumerated in the Index, age was specified for 7,063.[8] Subtracting 287 from 7,063 left 6,776 delinquents who were reported to the Index for offenses not involving vandalism.

The mean age for the 287 vandals was 12.94 years. The mean age for the 6,776 other delinquents was 14.46 years, or 1.52 years more than the mean age of the vandals.

Table II compares the age distribution of the Bronx vandals with the age distribution of the Bronx delinquents reported for

TABLE II
NUMBERS AND PERCENTAGES OF VANDALS AND OTHER DELINQUENTS, BY AGE, THE BRONX, NEW YORK CITY, 1955

	Vandals 6-20 Years Old		*Other Delinquents 6-20 Years Old*		*Difference*
Age	*Number*	*Per Cent*	*Number*	*Per Cent*	*Per Cent*
6- 8 Years	23	8.0	248	3.7	4.3
9-11 Years	74	25.8	805	11.9	13.9
12-14 Years	90	31.3	2,097	30.9	.4
15-17 Years	86	30.0	2,661	39.3	- 9.3
18-20 Years	14	4.9	965	14.2	- 9.3
TOTAL	287	100.0	6,776	100.0	

Mean = 12.94 Mean = 14.46
S.D. = ±3.10 S.D. = ±2.99
C.R. = 8.13; $P < .05$

Source: Juvenile Delinquency Index, New York City Youth Board, 1955.

[6] *A Study of Vandalism.* Denver, Denver Area Welfare Council, April, 1954, p. 5.

[7] W. H. Clark: Sex differences and motivation in the urge to destroy. *The Journal of Social Psychology,* 36 (November, 1952), pp. 167-177.

[8] *Juvenile Delinquency Profile: 1955, New York City, op. cit.,* Table 12, p. 13.

offenses other than vandalism. It should be noted that, although the age distribution of the vandals roughly paralleled the age distribution of the other delinquents, at the *.05 level of significance* the mean age of the vandals (12.94 years) was less than the mean age of the other delinquents (14.46 years).

Adolescence may be defined as the period twelve through twenty years of age and pre-adolescence or childhood may be defined as the period six through eleven years of age. According to these definitions, 66.2 per cent of the vandals were adolescents, with 34.9 per cent of them fifteen or more years of age; 84.4 per cent of the other delinquents were adolescents, with 53.5 per cent of them fifteen or more years of age; 33.8 per cent of the vandals were pre-adolescents, compared with only 15.6 per cent of the other delinquents.

Thus, while the majority of both the vandals and the other delinquents were adolescents, substantially more of the vandals were pre-adolescents, while substantially fewer of them were fifteen or more years of age.

Although these results disagree with suggestions in the literature that most vandals are fifteen to twenty-one years of age,[9] they are in general agreement with the suggestion that vandalism is mainly the behavior of children and adolescents[10] and that, as was found in the Denver study, such destruction is particularly characteristic of the early and mid-adolescent years.[11]

Ethnic Characteristics

Ethnic group membership was specified for 280 of the 291 Bronx vandals. Of the 7,112 Bronx delinquents enumerated in the Index, ethnic group was specified for 6,946.[12] Subtracting 280

---

[9] R. V. Merry: Vandalism. *Encyclopedia of Modern Education.* New York, The Philosophical Library of New York City, 1943, pp. 873-874; Baboons or barbarians?, *Scholastic,* 33 (October 29, 1938), p. 2.

[10] H. S. Dewhurst: *The Railroad Police.* Springfield, Illinois, Charles C Thomas, Publisher, 1955, pp. 114-116.

[11] *A Study of Vandalism, op. cit.,* pp. 5 and 15; also B. Solomon: Vandalism. *Youth Leaders Digest,* 17 (February, 1955), p. 162.

[12] *Juvenile Delinquency Profile: 1955, New York City, op. cit.,* Table 13, p. 14.

from 6,946 left 6,666 delinquents who were reported to the Index for offenses not involving vandalism.

Table III compares the ethnic distribution of the Bronx vandals with the ethnic distribution of the Bronx delinquents reported for offenses other than vandalism. It should be noted that, although the ethnic distribution of the vandals paralleled the ethnic distribution of the other delinquents, at the *.05 level of significance* a higher proportion of the vandals were white (67.8% to 62.3%); a lower proportion were non-white (16.8% to 23.7%); while a slightly higher proportion were Puerto Rican (15.4% to 14.0%).

TABLE III

NUMBERS AND PERCENTAGES OF VANDALS AND OTHER DELINQUENTS BY ETHNIC GROUP, THE BRONX, NEW YORK CITY, 1955

Ethnic Group	*Vandals 6-20 Years Old* Number	*Vandals 6-20 Years Old* Per Cent	*Other Delinquents 6-20 Years Old* Number	*Other Delinquents 6-20 Years Old* Per Cent	*Difference* Per Cent
White	190	67.8	4,152	62.3	5.5
Non-White	47	16.8	1,583	23.7	– 6.9
Puerto Rican	43	15.4	931	14.0	1.4
TOTAL	280	100.0	6,666	100.0	

$X^2 = 7.25$; $P < .05$

Source: Juvenile Delinquency Index, New York City Youth Board, 1955.

Thus, compared with the other delinquents, whites were over-represented among the vandals, non-whites were under-represented, while Puerto Ricans were slightly over-represented.

Although there is very little suggestion in the literature regarding the ethnic characteristics of vandals, these results do not support the suggestion offered by Clinard and Wade that it is unlikely that vandalism is more typical of certain racial or ethnic groups than others.[13]

Socio-Economic Characteristics

Neighborhood of residence has long been recognized as an indicator of social class position. Geographically, New York City is divided into statistical units known as health areas for which

[13] Clinard and Wade, *op. cit.*

statistics on population, morbidity, and mortality have been collected for over two decades. In 1950 the Bronx was divided into sixty-five such areas.

According to the New York Tuberculosis and Health Association, "The association of tuberculosis and environment, social, economic and physical has been recognized and to some degree recorded in New York City for almost a century."[14]

In the present study the array of the sixty-five Bronx health areas, arranged according to the decreasing order of the magnitude of their "tuberculosis prevalence rates" for the three-year period 1949-1951, was used as a basis for ranking such areas according to their socio-economic level.[15]

The array of health areas was then subdivided into quartiles with the highest quarter representing the sixteen areas of *lowest* socio-economic level; the second highest quarter representing the sixteen areas of *second lowest* socio-economic level; the third highest quarter representing the sixteen areas of *third lowest* socio-economic level; and the lowest quarter representing the sixteen[16] areas of *highest* socio-economic level.

The 1950 U. S. Census reported that 288,706 individuals, six through twenty years of age, lived in the Bronx.[17] Tabulation of this population by health area quartiles revealed that 26.8 per cent lived in the sixteen areas of lowest socio-economic level; 19.9 per cent in the sixteen areas of second lowest socio-economic level; 23.8 per cent in the sixteen areas of third lowest socio-economic level; and 29.5 per cent in the sixteen areas of highest socio-economic level.

---

[14] A. M. Lowell: *Socio-Economic Conditions and Tuberculosis, New York City, 1949-1951*. New York, New York Tuberculosis and Health Association, 1956, p. 4.

[15] For the Bronx health areas, the tuberculosis prevalence rate for the period 1949-1951 (representing the yearly average for the three years 1949, 1950 and 1951 of the known tuberculosis cases per 100,000 population) had good coefficients of correlation with the proportion of dwelling units in dilapidated condition or with inadequate plumbing in 1950 (r +.53), with median family income in 1949 (r −.79), and with the proportion of population white, excluding Puerto Ricans, in 1950 (r −.86). *Ibid.*, Table A, p. 35.

[16] Health area #48 (Riker's Island), the seventeenth health area falling in the lowest quarter, was omitted. The population of this area was composed of the inmates and personnel at the Riker's Island Penitentiary.

[17] *Juvenile Delinquency Profile: 1955, New York City, op. cit.*, Table 2, pp. 23-24.

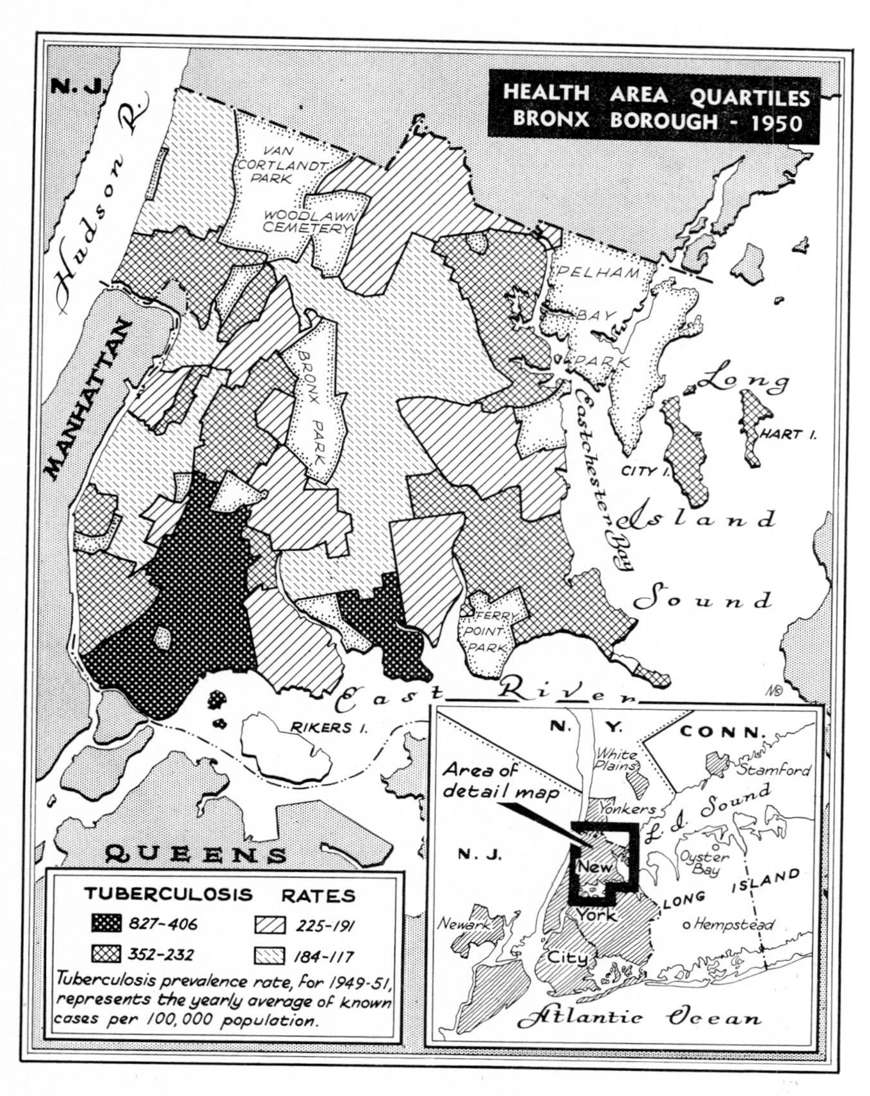

Bronx Borough, New York City, 1950, Showing Health Area Quartiles Plotted According to Their Tuberculosis Prevalence Rates

Health area of residence was specified for 283 of the 291 Bronx vandals reported to the Juvenile Delinquency Index in 1955. Of the 7,112 Bronx delinquents reported to the Index in 1955, health area of residence was specified for 6,808.[18] When correction was made for twelve delinquents who resided on Riker's Island, this total became 6,796. Subtracting 283 from 6,796 left 6,513 Bronx delinquents who were reported to the Index for offenses not involving vandalism.

Table IV compares the health area distribution of the Bronx vandals with the health area distribution of the Bronx delinquents reported for offenses other than vandalism. It should be noted that, at the *.05 level of significance,* no difference existed between the distribution of the vandals and the distribution of the other delinquents. While 48.0 per cent of the vandals and 48.9 per cent of the other delinquents lived in the sixteen areas of lowest socio-economic level, both the percentage of vandals and the percentage of other delinquents uniformly increased as the socio-economic level of the health area quartiles decreased.

TABLE IV

NUMBERS AND PERCENTAGES OF VANDALS AND OTHER DELINQUENTS, BY HEALTH AREA QUARTILES GROUPED ON THE BASIS OF HEALTH AREA TUBERCULOSIS PREVALENCE RATES (1949-1951), THE BRONX, NEW YORK CITY, 1955

Quartile Grouping of 64 Bronx Health Areas	*Vandals 6-20 Years Old†*		*Other Delinquents 6-20 Years Old†*		*Difference*
	Number	*Per Cent*	*Number*	*Per Cent*	*Per Cent*
Highest Quarter (TB Rates 827-406)	136	48.0	3,186	48.9	– .9
2nd Highest Quarter (TB Rates 352-232)	58	20.5	1,284	19.7	.8
3rd Highest Quarter (TB Rates 225-191)	50	17.7	1,051	16.2	1.5
Lowest Quarter* (TB Rates 184-117)	39	13.8	992	15.2	–1.4
TOTAL	283	100.0	6,513	100.0	

$X^2 = 0.90; P > .05$

* Health area #48 (Riker's Island) omitted.

† Source: Juvenile Delinquency Index, New York City Youth Board, 1955.

[18] *Ibid.,* Table 1, pp. 20-22.

Thus, while the distribution of the general Bronx child population, six through twenty years of age, as reported in the 1950 U. S. Census, showed no marked tendency to vary uniformly according to the socio-economic level of the areas in which they lived, both the distribution of the vandals and the distribution of the other delinquents uniformly increased as socio-economic level decreased. Almost one-half of both the vandals and the other delinquents lived in the areas of lowest socio-economic level.

These results do not support the sometimes-expressed belief that vandalism is more prevalent among middle-class children.[19] They do support suggestions that vandals are drawn from a variety of class levels,[20] and in particular the conclusion reached in the study of vandalism in Denver that, while most of the vandals studied lived in low-income areas, enough exceptions existed to dispel any theory that only children from low-income families tended to commit acts of vandalism.[21]

OTHER CHARACTERISTICS OF VANDALS

In New York City exclusive jurisdiction over allegedly delinquent children under sixteen years of age is given to the Children's Court Division of the New York City Domestic Relations Court. At the discretion of the criminal courts special procedure is provided for transfer to the Children's Court of fifteen-year-old children who are accused of crimes punishable by death or life imprisonment. One or more Parts of the Children's Court are set up in each of the five boroughs of the city.

During 1955 a total of 1,571 new cases appeared before the Bronx Children's Court because of their alleged delinquent behavior.[22] Forty-three, or 2.7 per cent, of this total appeared for

---

[19] Vandalism: A major child behavior problem. *Science Digest,* 33 (January, 1953), p. 38.

[20] F. Otwell: What price vandalism? *Bus Transportation,* 30 (March, 1951), pp. 27-29; A. Usher: Vandals, or just kids? *Better Homes and Gardens,* 31 (November, 1953), p. 30; S. L. Gingery: Vandalism in schools. *School Business Affairs,* 12 (September, 1956), p. 5.

[21] *A Study of Vandalism, op. cit.,* p. 7.

[22] *Twenty-third Annual Report of the Domestic Relations Court of the City of New York, 1955.* New York, Domestic Relations Court, City of New York, 1956, Part II, Table 9, p. 9.

offenses involving vandalism. Of these forty-three cases, thirty were actually adjudicated delinquent, and of these, twenty-nine were residents of the Bronx.

These twenty-nine cases will be examined in detail in Chapter III. In the present section, comparisons between several of the characteristics of these cases and the characteristics of other delinquent populations described in the literature will be made for the purpose of further suggesting how vandals may differ from other delinquents.

Comparison of the Bronx Children's Court vandals with other delinquent populations suggested that the families of vandals may be characterized by more parent-child conflict and hostility than the families of other delinquents. Thus, while only 22 per cent of the delinquent boys studied by William C. Kvaraceus at the Passaic, New Jersey, Children's Bureau, were noted to have come from homes characterized by family-child conflict,[23] 62 per cent of the Bronx vandals came from families characterized by parent-child conflict and tension.

Comparison between the Bronx Children's Court vandals and the five hundred Boston delinquents studied by Sheldon and Eleanor Glueck in *Unraveling Juvenile Delinquency* indicated that the families of vandals may be much less mobile than the families of other delinquents. Whereas only 3 per cent of the Bronx vandals had lived at their present addresses for less than one year, 33.6 per cent of the Boston delinquents had lived at their present addresses for less than one year; and whereas 59 per cent of the Bronx vandals had lived at their present addresses for eight or more years, only 11.4 per cent of the Boston delinquents had lived at their present addresses for eight years or more.[24]

Finally, when the percentage of Bronx vandals who had committed their offenses alone was compared with the percentage of youngsters among a group of male delinquents in Chicago, studied by Shaw and McKay, who had committed their delinquency alone, the results suggested that vandalism is even more

---

[23] W. C. Kvaraceus: *Juvenile Delinquency and the School.* Yonkers-on-Hudson, New York, World Book Company, 1945, pp. 74-75.

[24] S. and E. Glueck: *Unraveling Juvenile Delinquency.* New York, The Commonwealth Fund, 1950, Table VIII-2, p. 80.

of a group offense than is other male delinquency. Thus, while only 4 per cent of twenty-eight of the Bronx vandals committed their property destruction alone, 18.2 per cent of 5,480 male delinquents who appeared in the Chicago juvenile court were reported to have committed their offenses alone.[25]

In sum, comparisons between Bronx vandals and other delinquents reported to the Juvenile Delinquency Index of the New York City Youth Board in 1955 indicated that, although both vandals and other kinds of delinquents appear to live largely in deteriorated neighborhoods, the "typical" vandal is otherwise considerably different from other delinquents. Compared with other delinquents, he is much more likely to be a male; he is apparently younger; and he is more likely to be white, less likely to be non-white, and only slightly more likely to be Puerto Rican.

Further comparisons between Bronx Children's Court vandals and other delinquent populations also suggested how vandals differ from other delinquents. Thus vandals are apparently more likely to come from homes characterized by parent-child conflict; their families are seemingly far less mobile than the families of other delinquents; and vandals appear much more likely to commit their property destruction in company with other youngsters.

---

[25] C. R. Shaw and H. D. McKay: *Social Factors in Juvenile Delinquency,* National Commission on Law Observance and Enforcement, Report on the Causes of Crime, Vol. II. Washington, Government Printing Office, 1931, pp. 194-195.

Chapter III

TYPES OF VANDALS

STUDENTS of the crime problem are especially fond of classifying offenders according to type. Traditionally one of the simplest distinctions made has been between felons and those guilty of lesser crimes. Another classification has distinguished three kinds of offenders: those who commit crimes against property, those who commit crimes against persons, and those who violate public order or who threaten the welfare of the state.

During recent times, taking their cue from the 19th-century Italian criminologist Cesare Lombroso, sociologists and others have frequently looked beyond the criminal act and considered the characteristics of offenders themselves. Thus, for example, some years ago Lindesmith and Dunham suggested that offenders might be classified on a continuum with the "social criminal" at one pole and the "individualized criminal" at the other. They considered the social criminal to be the offender whose criminal behavior was supported and prescribed by his cultural milieu, while the individualized criminal was the one whose law violation was not so supported and prescribed, but who was deviant because of his mental pathology or because of the stress of a particular situation.[1]

More recently Marshall B. Clinard in his *Sociology of Deviant Behavior* described a similar continuum when he distinguished between the "individual" and the "career" types of criminals. At one end of his continuum Clinard placed the criminally insane and at the other, professional criminals such as pickpockets and

---

[1] A. R. Lindesmith and H. W. Dunham: Some principles of criminal typology. *Social Forces,* 19 (March, 1941), pp. 307-314.

confidence men. Between the two he located various other kinds of offenders.[2]

Similar differences have been noted among juvenile delinquents as distinct from law violators in general. Several years ago, for example, John B. Mays, a settlement house worker in a British slum, urged that we must discriminate between two general types of juvenile offenders: emotionally maladjusted "criminals" and environmental "delinquents." Although Mays thought the two types often merged and overlapped at many points, nevertheless he felt that emotional maladjustment was the key to understanding chronically deviant juvenile "criminals," while a delinquency-prone cultural background was the basic characteristic of the more frequently short-term, but more numerous, juvenile "delinquents."[3]

One of the most recent schemes for classifying child offenders appeared in a report published by the Juvenile Delinquency Project of the National Education Association.[4] This report attempted to present in summary form an integrated theory on delinquency and grew out of the thinking of a team of authorities on cultural anthropology, criminology, sociology, psychology, psychiatry, and pediatrics. Kvaraceus, the psychologist of the team, and his collaborators indicated that in terms of two variables—delinquency and emotional disturbance—the general child population could be classified according to four subtypes:

The "Normal" Youngster
The "Delinquent" Youngster with Little or No Emotional Disturbance
The "Delinquent" and "Disturbed" Youngster
The "Disturbed" but Not "Delinquent" Youngster

The NEA report suggested that of these four subtypes the first three are significant for an understanding of delinquency. The first type of youngster, comprising the great bulk of the

---

[2] M. B. Clinard: *Sociology of Deviant Behavior.* New York, Rinehart and Company, 1957, pp. 200-210.

[3] J. B. Mays: *Growing Up in the City.* Liverpool, Liverpool University Press, 1954, pp. 17-20.

[4] W. C. Kvaraceus, *et al.*: *Delinquent Behavior: Culture and the Individual.* Washington, National Education Association of the United States, 1959, chap. 7.

child population, generally is mentally and emotionally "normal" and, although occasionally engaging in minor mischief, essentially is not a delinquent. The second type, embracing the great bulk of the delinquent population, is severely delinquent not because of personal pathology, but because of cultural background. Kvaraceus and his associates noted that the majority of the boys and girls in this second type usually live in lower-class neighborhoods and reflect the delinquency characteristics of their immediate life situation. The third type of child is delinquent chiefly because of his mental and emotional disturbance, although his cultural background may also be involved. The fourth type is of public concern because of his mental disturbance, but since he seldom if ever violates legal or social norms, he is not properly considered a delinquent.

This chapter will suggest a descriptive typology of vandals derived from the intensive case study of the Bronx vandals, briefly described in Chapter II, who were adjudicated delinquent by the Children's Court in 1955. The typology to be presented is entirely in keeping with the distinction between "individual" and "social" or "career" offenders drawn in the various schemes described above, and in particular it closely parallels the classification of delinquents offered by Kvaraceus and his associates in the NEA report previously mentioned.

Children's Court records, including the results of available psychological and psychiatric examinations, provided the foundations upon which the case studies of vandals were constructed. In many of the cases much supplementary information was gathered from the records of public and parochial schools, state hospitals, correctional institutions, and other social agencies. In addition, in all but a few cases, "unstructured" interviews, frequently tape recorded, were held with the vandals themselves, their victims, members of their families and friends, as well as with various social workers, psychiatrists, school teachers and others to whom the vandals were known. Finally, the author personally observed the neighborhoods in which the children studied lived in order to augment information secured from other sources.

All typologies are vulnerable to those who wish to disagree, and typologies of criminals and delinquents are no exceptions. Nevertheless, the classification of law violators into subtypes often serves a highly useful function not performed by points of view which fail to distinguish categories of offenders. By dividing offenders into subtypes, thereby differentiating categories of offenders, we see that the roots of crime are quite dissimilar in each category and that the problems of prevention and control are also different for each category. The typology of vandalism presented below makes these distinctions.

Of the twenty-nine Bronx vandals adjudicated delinquent by the Children's Court in 1955, twenty-seven could be classified according to three different, albeit not entirely distinct, subtypes: *Disturbed Vandals, Essentially Law-Abiding Vandals,* and *Sub-cultural Vandals.* Two of the twenty-nine boys could not be classified because of insufficient information.

DISTURBED VANDALS

Four of the cases were placed in this category. Two were Negro boys, eleven and twelve years of age, born in metropolitan New York of native-born parents. Two were Puerto Rican boys, also eleven and twelve years of age, who had migrated from the Island with their mothers. All lived in economically deprived homes located in underprivileged and delinquency-prone neighborhoods. Three came from permanently broken homes and all came from families characterized by parent-child tension and conflict, frequently involving the ineffectual attempts of parents to regulate the behavior of their children. All were truants and were otherwise poorly adjusted in school. Only one was a church member. All had committed other delinquencies, including other acts of vandalism, either before or soon after their court appearance. All had been in the company of other boys when they committed the vandalism which brought them to court. In addition, two of the boys appeared to have had some sort of affiliation with loosely-knit neighborhood gangs.

Within some two years after their court appearances, three of the four boys placed in this category had been committed to mental hospitals where each was found to be suffering from a "psychotic disorder" of the schizophrenic type. Prior to his court appearance, one of the three had similarly been confined for a time with the same type of disorder. Prior to his appearance, the fourth boy, after threatening suicide, had been committed to a mental hospital for observation. At that time it was suggested that he was probably schizophrenic. After his court appearance he was again committed for observation and found to be characterized by a "personality disorder." When he was later committed to a state institution for delinquents, the staff noted that he stayed mostly to himself and appeared to live in a world of fantasy. When first committed to the state school, a staff psychiatrist reported that, although a diagnosis of schizophrenia seemed unwarranted, the boy's behavior did include a disintegration pattern which might justify such a diagnosis.

Intelligence tests indicated that all four boys were functioning at less than the "average" intellectual level: two were "dull and backward" and two were mildly "feebleminded."

The following case illustrates the kind of vandal placed in this category. It clearly describes the progressive mental deterioration characteristic of such youngsters. It also shows how vandalism is only one facet of the massively disordered, delinquent, and rootless lives such boys live, largely isolated from family, school, other community institutions, and sometimes even friends. As such it is a fine example of what Dunham has called "the schizophrene as a social type."[5] The case exemplifies, as well, "the psychotic reaction pattern" which the Swiss psychiatrist Bovet has suggested may develop when the suitably predisposed children of immigrants to the United States "fall victims of a conflict between the culture of their native countries and the culture of this new civilization to which they must adapt themselves in the pitiless struggle for existence."[6]

Case One: Adrift in Nueva York

Juan was born in Ponce, Puerto Rico, while his mother, a woman with a fifth-grade education, lived for a time in a con-

---

[5] H. W. Dunham: The schizophrene and criminal behavior. *American Sociological Review*, 4 (June, 1939), pp. 352-361.

[6] L. Bovet: *Psychiatric Aspects of Juvenile Delinquency.* Geneva, World Health Organization, 1951, p. 37.

sensual relationship[7] with his father. A sister, now deceased, was also born of this union. Prior to living with Juan's father, the mother, starting when she was fourteen years old, had lived with another man for a year or two in a similar relationship from which two children had also resulted. One is now deceased. The other is Manuel, Juan's half-brother.

When Juan was four years old, his mother came to New York City seeking employment. Originally she came alone, but after securing employment in the needle trades industry, sent for her children.

Little is known of Juan until he was six years of age when he entered public school in the Bronx. Almost from the beginning his teachers found him to be a nervous child with peculiar mannerisms. By the time he was eight years old his erratic conduct in school caused him to be referred for examination by school psychologists. He was found to be an intellectually dull boy, but test results were regarded as "minimal" in terms of his actual potential. He was fairly fluent in English. His mother reported that she was very much concerned for his welfare, that she personally took him to and from school, that she guarded his out-of-school activities very closely, and that she only permitted him to play outdoors when she was around to supervise him. She said that she was cautious because of his chronic asthma which he had had since he was two years old.

Two years after this first examination, Juan was again referred to school psychologists because of his foolishness and poor adjustment in school. He was found to be an obese, sluggish, emotionally flat, fourth-grade boy who was unable to participate in class work, was disturbed in school—making noises, covering his head with his hands and talking to himself—and who would not come to school at all unless his mother brought him. In contrast with his first examination, he was found to be mildly feebleminded and had poor language development not only in English, but also in Spanish. He was practically a nonreader who could not print or write his name. As a result of

---

[7] Consensual or common-law marriage is an important characteristic of Puerto Rican family life, especially among lower-class people. Estimates have varied, but at least twenty-five per cent of all marriages on the Island appear to be of this type. Cf. C. W. Mills, *et al.: The Puerto Rican Journey.* New York, Harper and Brothers, 1950, p. 9; P. J. Reiss: Backgrounds of Puerto Rican delinquency in New York City. Unpublished Master's thesis, Fordham University, New York, 1953, p. 50.

this examination, the boy was found eligible for a retarded class and so placed.

Shortly before his second psychological examination, Juan had been sent to a Referral Unit of the New York City Youth Board because of his poor school adjustment. Juan's mother told his Youth Board worker that she was very anxious about him and that she feared he would run away. Sometimes, she said, she would put a dress on him to keep him in the house. The mother admitted that she had little control over the boy, that she felt helpless, and that she frequently had to ask neighbors to discipline her son.

While Juan was on referral to the Youth Board, and a few weeks before he was first brought to Children's Court for delinquency, his mother was committed to a mental hospital as the result of a long-standing emotional disturbance, diagnosed as "Dementia Praecox, Catatonic Type,"[8] and the maternal grandmother, an elderly and feeble person, took over care of Juan.

Almost immediately Juan was arrested for car theft and referred to Children's Court where he was discharged with a warning. The grandmother admitted to a court probation officer that she too had little control over the boy who lived with her in a furnished room in a changing neighborhood in the lower Bronx where the population was rapidly shifting from predominantly Jewish and Irish families to Puerto Rican and Negro. However, the grandmother was opposed to placement for the boy, since she was afraid of the effect this would have on Juan's mother.

The probation officer also noted that Juan was continuing to

---

[8] The development of a severe mental disorder by both Juan and his mother is in itself a noteworthy characteristic in this case. This phenomenon, sometimes called "the psychosis of association" *(folie à deux)*, has been described as the condition, chiefly occurring among family members, wherein one disordered person is influenced by intimate association with another person who is also disordered. Cf. A. Gralnick: *Folie à deux*—The psychosis of association. *Psychiatric Quarterly*, 16 (April and July, 1942), pp. 230-263; 491-520.

In connection with this case it is also interesting to note that, according to a New York City Children's Court psychiatrist, a random sampling of the parents of delinquent children coming to the Court showed that 10 per cent had one or both parents "insane," while another study found that an even greater number of such children had "at least one parent with serious emotional or intellectual defects." M. Rittwagen: *Sins of Their Fathers*. Boston, Houghton Mifflin Company, 1958, p. 42.

have difficulty in school and that, although he had been baptized Roman Catholic when an infant in Puerto Rico, in New York he was a nominal Catholic who seldom attended what Juan later described as "the English Mass." The probation officer further noted that Juan appeared to have little insight into his delinquency.

Shortly after Juan's court appearance, his grandmother told a worker in the Department of Welfare, from which she was receiving financial assistance for the boy, that although she was still having difficulty in supervising the child, she still would not accept placement for him—again because of her fear of her daughter's reaction. The Department of Welfare worker also had difficulty in explaining the compulsory school attendance law to the grandmother, who felt that since Juan did not like school, he should not be forced to attend.

Six months after his first court appearance Juan was again brought to court, this time on petition of his grandmother, with whom he was still living. He had stolen $32.00 from her, bought a bicycle from a Western Union boy, and used it to run away from home. He was placed in detention at Youth House where he told his social worker that his grandmother, whom he called "mother," was a "policewoman." He said that he ran away because his half-brother Manuel, who lived in the same rooming house as did Juan and his grandmother, and who also had a history of delinquency, used to beat him to discipline him, usually at the grandmother's request. Juan further told the worker that he had warned his grandmother that he would run away if Manuel, whom he hated, continued to beat him. He said that his grandmother had not believed him, so he ran away to show her that he had meant it. The worker noted that Juan showed no remorse for stealing the money and that he told, "with shining eyes," a tale filled with fantasy of running away on his bicycle to "Canada" (actually New Jersey) with a friend. The worker also noted that Juan had expressed the wish that the court place him outside of his own home, because if he returned, he would again do "bad things."

While at Youth House, Juan impressed the staff as a "friendly" and "jolly" boy who was well liked by his peers, although they laughed at him because of his obesity. The staff also noted he impressed them as being a boy who was "not emotionally close to anyone."

While Juan was before the court on his grandmother's petition, the Department of Welfare made an urgent request that the boy be placed outside the home. However, the court was unable to arrange such placement and Juan was returned to live with his grandmother.

Three months after his return Juan was suspended from school. His truancy had continued and when in school he was constantly in difficulty. Immediately prior to his suspension he had disrupted the class, shouted profanity in Spanish at the teacher, invited other boys in the class to accompany him to "Woolworth's" where he would show them how to steal merchandise, wore his roller skates to school and refused to take them off, insisted on wearing his hat all the time and caused a near riot in the girls' yard.

Five days after his suspension Juan committed his vandalism, which brought him to court for the third time. This occurred when he was twelve years old. He and two other Puerto Rican boys broke the windows in the apartment of a rabbi living in their neighborhood. The three boys had done the same thing on a number of other occasions during the preceding weeks, but had not been apprehended.

When questioned about his vandalism, Juan told his probation officer that he did not like Jewish people. Later, detached and vague of manner, he said that he and other boys had thrown bottles through the window of "a Jew." He continued by describing, gleefully, how they had done this on several other occasions and that "the Jew" would chase them, but was unable to catch them.

Although streets gangs existed in Juan's neighborhood, he denied that he belonged to any such group and no evidence to the contrary was developed. Juan used to play on the streets, in the parks, and along the railroad tracks in the company of the other boys, but more usually he wandered about the city on his own, frequently astride his bicycle.

As the result of his vandalism, Juan was committed to a state training school where his progress was described as "slow." He made several attempts to run away and made little progress in academic work. He was released from the school after an eighteen-month stay to live with his grandmother and mother who, meanwhile, had been released from her mental hospital on convalescent status.

Fifteen months after he was released from the training school Juan was committed to a state hospital after he had again been brought to Children's Court, this time for breaking into an apartment with another Puerto Rican boy. The court sent him to Bellevue Hospital for observation because of his obviously disturbed state. At Bellevue he was found to be very disturbed, suicidal, homicidal, paranoid, and hallucinated. From Bellevue he was committed to a state mental hospital where he was diagnosed as "Dementia Praecox, Paranoid Type."

At first Juan made a precarious adjustment at the hospital. Later his behavior became more satisfactory. However, after a lapse of a few months, he became involved in petty pilfering, and assaultive and threatening to the staff. He assaulted one attendant, threatened to kill a physician, supervisor, and another attendant. On one occasion, armed with an eating fork, he ran amuck and had to be subdued by five attendants.

At fifteen, he continues to be confined to the hospital under close security.

ESSENTIALLY LAW-ABIDING VANDALS

Five boys were placed in this category. Four were white children born in metropolitan New York of native-born parents. One was a Puerto Rican boy who had migrated from the Island with his family. The five ranged from nine through fifteen years of age, but the majority were thirteen or more years old. Only the Puerto Rican boy lived in an underprivileged and delinquency-prone neighborhood. The others lived in better neighborhoods; indeed the neighborhoods in which most lived were, socially and economically, among the best in the Bronx. All the boys placed in this category came from intact homes with comparatively little parent-child tension and conflict. All but one boy were affiliated with a church or synagogue. Most had made fairly poor adjustments at school, but only one had been a truant. Otherwise none had been previously delinquent and none had again been delinquent within some two years after his court appearance. Although the vandalism which brought each to court had been committed in company with other boys, none of the five had a gang affiliation.

Finally, the behavior of only two of the boys had caused them to be referred for psychiatric examination, and neither was found to be psychotic or near-psychotic, although both were thought to be characterized by "personality disorders."

Test results available on all but one boy indicated that, although one was of "average or better" intelligence, two of the others were mildly "feebleminded," while the last was "dull and backward."

The next case illustrates the relatively well-ordered social relationships generally characteristic of the boys labeled Essentially Law-Abiding Vandals and, as measured by their total life pattern, the incidental, sometimes entirely fortuitous, nature of their delinquency. The case also portrays the happy combination of circumstances wherein stable and resourceful parents, amply supported by school, church, and closely-knit "consanguine" family relationships in an ethnic community,[9] can first shelter and then entirely remove an accepting child from contact and participation in the gang delinquency which claims other children in their neighborhood. Furthermore, the case shows the role organized recreation may play in satisfying the needs of the gregarious child who, unable to make academic progress in school, might otherwise seek satisfaction in the delinquent companionship readily available in his neighborhood.

Although there appears to be no necessary relationship between quantitative intelligence and delinquency,[10] the case is also suggestive of the manner in which mentally deficient children may become involved in delinquency as pawns in the hands of older, more sophisticated acquaintances.

Case Two: The Dupe

Joey's mother and father are people of Italian descent. They were born and raised in the same neighborhood in which they

[9] For a discussion of the function of the ethnic community in preventing personal and social disorganization among its members as they assimilate into American society, see J. P. Fitzpatrick: The integration of Puerto Ricans. *Thought,* 30 (Autumn, 1955), pp. 402-420.

[10] For a discussion of this point, see H. A. Bloch and F. T. Flynn: *Delinquency: The Juvenile Offender in America Today.* New York, Random House, 1956, pp. 115-122.

lived until after Joey appeared in Children's Court for being involved in school vandalism when he was nine years old. This neighborhood, complete with candy stores and store-front social and athletic clubs, is in an old established section of the central Bronx, commonly known as "Little Italy," notorious for its street gangs and underworld activity, including professional gangland killings. An observer of the area described it as a "more or less static" community "one step above the slums." Few Puerto Ricans or Negroes actually live in the area. However, considerable tension exists between the residents and Puerto Ricans and Negroes who heavily populate nearby areas. Fights between Puerto Rican boys and boys from the neighborhood are fairly common and shortly after Joey appeared in court, local boys stoned the house of a Negro family which had newly settled in Joey's neighborhood. When meetings were held by interested social agencies to discuss solutions to such stonings, some of the residents seriously proposed that "boundary lines" be established around the area which no Negroes or Puerto Ricans would be allowed to cross.

Joey, a mildly feebleminded, but docile and friendly boy, was brought to court for the first and only time after he and seven older boys had been involved in vandalism at the neighborhood public school. This school had traditionally been broken into by local children and youths, frequently because of their desire to loot, and especially because of their desire to swim in the school pool.

Joey's mother, a woman with a grammar school education, married his father, a high school graduate, at the parish church eleven years before Joey was born. After the marriage, the father had been steadily employed as a painter, while the mother remained at home as a housewife. The family always maintained close relationships with nearby relatives. The intrafamilial relationships were also intimate and harmonious, with the father benevolently playing the dominant role. Both parents were always extremely cautious in their supervision of Joey, keeping him at home in the evening and not permitting him to roam the streets at night as was the custom for other boys in the neighborhood. The family had always been self-supporting and had had no contact with the police, courts, or social agencies except for its brief contact with the Children's Court when Joey was found delinquent and dismissed by the court with a warning.

Although Joey's mother and father were irregular in their church attendance, Joey attended church regularly.

When asked about what he liked to do, Joey said that he was very much interested in baseball, although he also enjoyed the skating parties sponsored by the parish. He further said that he liked to watch television, attend movies, ride his bicycle and play with his cousins and other friends. When he grew up, he said, he would like to be a baseball player, like Willie Mays, or "anybody, as long as I'm in the major leagues."

When asked if he got along well with his father, Joey said, in a simple manner, "Of course, he's my father." About his mother he said, "I like her too."

Joey entered kindergarten at the parish school and remained there through the third grade. He then transferred to the public school which was located directly across the street from his home. It was at this school that the vandalism occurred. In public school Joey was examined by psychologists and placed in a retarded class. This displeased his father, who thereupon had him transferred back to the parish school, where, as the father phrased it, Joey "not only received regular school work, but also received religious training and proper discipline when he needed it." The father admitted, however, that even though Joey was unable to read, he had been promoted as far as the seventh grade at the parish school. In school Joey had never been a behavior problem, getting along well with both teachers and other pupils. At public school he was a "patrol boy," and after he returned to the parish school, played on one of the softball teams and won a trophy of which he was very proud.

Both Joey and his parents were concerned about his inability to read. Joey expressed his concern by saying, "They say if you don't know how to read, you can't become a baseball player. 'Cause if you become a baseball player you have to go to college sometimes." When asked if he would like to go to college, he replied, "If that would help me become a baseball player."

When asked, Joey explained his preference for the parish school in the following words, " 'Cause at the Catlik schools they teach better. You learn better. . . . When the teacher (at P.S. 532) she goes out of the room, everybody talks. But in San Gennaro's, if you start to talk, you're gonna get it! So nobody talks. You just keep quiet and mind your own business and do your work. In P.S. 532 they fight."

Joey explained his involvement in the vandalism which brought him to Children's Court in the following manner. "I was playin' ball with my friends and they (the older boys involved in the vandalism) wanted to go into the school. It was a hot day. So they called me—first they called one boy, but he wasn't in it. He went away 'cause he didn't want to go in there —so they called me and I kept sayin', 'no, no, no.' But they boost me in the winda . . . and I went in the winda. I cudn't come out the winda . . . so I hadda go through the door. So I went through the door and they went in (through the opened door). And I went back to playin' ball. And the next day, when I went to school, the principal, Miss—I forget her name—she grabbed me and she brought me in the room and she started talkin' about the day we broke into the school. So that's all. And that's how it happened." When asked if he had stayed in the school with the older boys, Joey said, "No, I didn't stay in. I saw them start to break things. So I went to play ball."

At the time Joey was adjudged delinquent, the investigating police officer substantially confirmed Joey's version of his offense. The officer informed the court that the boy "had been duped into being pushed through the window" by the "ringleader" of the group of older boys involved in the incident.

Most of the older boys involved with Joey in his delinquency later became part of an Italian street gang called the Dudes, well known for their delinquency, including their fights with the Sculpins, a group of Puerto Rican boys living nearby. Joey, however, never became a member of the Dudes or any other gang. Nor has he ever been involved in difficulties with the police or apparently anyone else, aside from his one offense. As Joey explained it at one time, "I get along with everybody."

Two years after his delinquency Joey and his family moved to a new duplex house shared with relatives in a more recently settled part of the east Bronx. The move was motivated by the father's concern for Joey, his only son. The father felt that even though he had raised two older daughters without difficulty in the central Bronx neighborhood, Joey—not because the father realized his son was feebleminded, but simply because he was a boy—would continue to get into trouble if he remained in the old neighborhood. Therefore, as the father put it, although he "couldn't really afford it," he moved to a better neighborhood.

The following case also illustrates the relatively well-ordered social relationships typical of Essentially Law-Abiding Vandals and the incidental nature of their delinquency. In contrast with the case just described, however, the family in this case did not face the problem of protecting a gregarious, mentally deficient son from the rigors of gang delinquency awaiting him in his neighborhood. Instead, this is the case of a precocious and somewhat withdrawn youngster who lived in a high-grade residential area. His problem appears to have stemmed not from involvement in neighborhood delinquency, but from the quality of his intrafamilial relationships, particularly rivalry with his brother, and from his inability to relate well with others, his dissatisfaction with school, and his continued conflict with school personnel.

The case is also suggestive of the highly effective role psychiatry may play in the adjustment of the intelligent and not grossly disturbed, middle-class child whose episodic delinquency is not supported by intimate association with delinquent peers.

Case Three: A Precocious Vandal

Sidney is a tall, glib, honor student at Bronx High School, reputed to be one of the best academic high schools in New York City. Intellectually, he is of superior intelligence and reads prodigiously in the fields of science, history, the arts, and especially in mathematics for which he has a particular aptitude. Athletically, he is more interested in competing on the school swimming team than in group sports such as basketball. He intends to attend college at Yale, or at another university with both a good academic standing and a swimming team, and then to work at "something in the field of mathematics." In the opinion of a psychiatrist who treated Sidney for a time, the boy has fine potentials as a scientist. "He's going places." However, Sidney did not always face such prospects. During his last year in public grammar school, when he was thirteen years of age, he was brought to Children's Court for the vandalism he committed in his school in company with another student.

Sidney is one of two children. His older brother, Irwin, is also an excellent student at the same high school. Irwin has never been in difficulty with the police. The father of the boys, a man with a grammar school education, owns a small business in the garment industry. The mother, a woman with some college education, works as a part-time bookkeeper in the father's business. Both parents were born in New York City and knew each other for a number of years prior to their marriage in a Jewish religious ceremony some eight years before Sidney's birth. Although Sidney's mother does not keep a kosher home, the family attends their synagogue during the High Holy Days.

Since Sidney was born the family has lived in a stable, predominantly Jewish neighborhood in one of the best sections of the west Bronx. Their home is a small, well-furnished apartment in a large, well-kept building in an area characterized by little delinquency.

The boy had made a poor social adjustment in school prior to committing his vandalism, the only offense for which he was known to the authorities. Although he was passing his course work and was not a truant, his conduct was consistently unsatisfactory. He refused to conform, was sullen and a disturbing influence in class, and critical and tormenting in his relationships with his teachers who tended to retaliate with hostility. He was in constant conflict with the school librarian who would not tolerate his keeping books overdue and who had forbidden him to borrow any more books. Sidney reacted to the librarian with considerable antagonism, believing that she acted "like the books were her own personal property" and that she was "badgering" him about overdue books.

As the result of his poor school adjustment, Sidney was brought to the attention of a Referral Unit of the New York City Youth Board which referred him for psychological examination. He was found to be a boy of superior intelligence, clandestinely hostile toward his parents and his brother, and with "few positive interests, limited inner resources, and with insufficient emotional interchange with others"—a boy who under stress "becomes more evasive and constricted and is finally likely to develop phobic, obsessive, or paranoid symptoms." Psychotherapy was recommended "to relax his defenses and gradually actualize his emotional and social potentials," preferably with a male therapist since he seemed "to be in search of a strong male figure with whom he can identify positively."

Eight months after this examination, Sidney committed the vandalism which brought him to Children's Court. While attending a night basketball game at his school, he invited a casual acquaintance, another Jewish boy who attended the same school, to explore deserted parts of the school with him. They entered the school library, using a key Sidney had in his possession, and proceeded to throw books about the room and upset bottles of ink over the librarian's desk. They then entered a classroom where Sidney wanted to erase some "demerits" from a teacher's record book. In the process of searching about the darkened room with the aid of matches, they accidentally started a small fire which they immediately extinguished. Before leaving the classroom, the boys found some crayons which they took with them.

In talking about his offense with his probation officer at Children's Court, Sidney said that he disliked the librarian and that his vandalism was as good an opportunity as any to "get back at her." In explaining why he had entered the classroom after he had been in the school library, Sidney said he wanted to remove demerits he had received because he was afraid they would hinder his entrance to the high school of his choice.

In explaining her boy's delinquency, Sidney's mother said that for some time before the delinquency rivalry existed between Sidney and his slightly older brother. Although both were bright boys, Sidney had not been able to gain the same "recognition" in grammar school his brother had received when he went to the same school. The mother said that Sidney had not found his classes very stimulating and that he had had some "trouble" with his teachers. As a result, she said, the boy's grades had suffered. On the other hand, her older son had always achieved good grades and Sidney, she said, had felt this keenly. When asked specifically about the librarian with whom Sidney had had difficulty, his mother said, "If you will pardon my expression, she was a 'bitch'! Always after the boys about one thing or another. We heard about her even before my two boys went to the school. Everybody had trouble with her."

The other boy involved with Sidney in the vandalism was named Phil. Just as with Sidney, this is the only offense for which Phil has been known to the authorities. However, unlike

Sidney, Phil was a mildly feebleminded boy who was thought to be functioning below his full intellectual potential. Although never a behavior problem in school, he had always had considerable academic difficulty. When asked why he had damaged the library with Sidney, Phil replied, in a courteous but rather bovine manner, that, finding himself before the deserted library in company with Sidney, who had a key to the door, he had said to himself, "This is your chance to get even." Questioned closely about this he explained by saying, "The librarian didn't like Jewish kids. She used to pull at the medals (hanging on a chain around their necks) when the kids came up to her desk. All the kids knew it. We even talked about it in class with one of the teachers." Phil readily admitted that he too had thrown books around the library and spilled ink on the librarian's desk, and that he had gone along with Sidney into the classroom which the boys had entered after leaving the library. They had been caught, Phil said, because Sidney "couldn't keep his mouth shut" about what they had done .

Immediately after their vandalism both boys were brought to Children's Court where, after psychiatric examination at the court clinic, both were placed on probation. Sidney was diagnosed as a "Schizoid Personality." He was found to be a boy who refused to "recognize his own individuality" and who tried to "copy his brother," who assumed the dominant role in their relationship. Although both boys had a number of friends, Sidney usually attached himself to his brother and to his brother's friends. As part of his probation plan, Sidney was referred for treatment to the Child Guidance Clinic at the Jewish Board of Guardians. His probation officer noted that the boy's mother seemed to be aware of his emotional difficulties and his need for psychiatric assistance, but that his father did not attach too much significance to his emotional problems, although he told the court he was willing to "go along" with clinical treatment and pay for such treatment if the court decided that it was necessary. The father also suggested that Sidney's difficulty stemmed from the fact that he was trying to compete with his brother. The probation officer further noted that both the mother and father appeared to be far more partial to their older son than to Sidney. He also stated that although Sidney had received religious instruction at *schul* until his *Bar Mitzvah,* his religious teachings and principles apparently had little effect upon his every-day behavior.

Although Sidney reported regularly to his probation officer, he never participated in treatment at the Jewish Board of Guardians. Instead his parents referred him to a distinguished New York psychiatrist, who found Sidney to be an intellectually "superior" child, but one who was culturally "stupid"—i.e., a child who had no appreciation of literature or the arts. He was a child who had simply not developed to anywhere near his full cultural potential, although, in the psychiatrist's opinion, he in no way suffered from a serious personality disturbance.

Sidney's treatment, to which he responded quickly, was predicated, said his psychiatrist, simply upon showing the boy that he was well liked. Later he introduced him to good poetry and literature, and brought him around to the point where he could see that "sex," about which he was much interested, but quite unsophisticated, was not just a physical act, but part of a mature and rewarding relationship with a woman.

As to Sidney's vandalism, the psychiatrist felt that the boy "wanted revenge on the school, then he was stupid enough to get caught." He believed that the boy "wanted to be a leader, but he could only lead in crime." As far as the vandalism went, treatment consisted of showing the boy that his delinquency was simply the act of a "show off," and in building up his self-image—e.g., by making him "proud of his looks."

The psychiatrist also believed that Sidney was not a "primitive type." He was not habitually malicious, nor could he ever physically assault anyone. He also thought that Sidney was not a boy whose personality would allow him to become part of a delinquent gang.

In a relatively short time, after his school adjustment had changed markedly, Sidney was discharged from treatment. Later he was also discharged from court supervision.

SUBCULTURAL VANDALS

Eighteen (two-thirds) of the twenty-seven boys examined were placed in this category. Sixteen were white and two were Negroes. All but one had been born in metropolitan New York. Most had native-born parents. In age the boys ranged from eight through fifteen years, but most were thirteen or more years old.

Although more than half of the boys lived in underprivileged and delinquency-prone neighborhoods, the others lived in better neighborhoods and one lived in one of the best areas in the Bronx. Although about half lived in economically deprived homes, only four came from permanently broken homes. However, the majority had families characterized by parent-child tension and conflict, usually involving the ineffectual attempts of parents to regulate the behavior of their children. All but two of the boys were members of a church congregation. About half had made poor adjustments at school and most had been truants.

All but one were known to have been delinquent before their court appearance or were again involved in delinquency within some two years after their appearance. Almost half had been previously involved in vandalism or were subsequently involved in such destruction. In all but one case the vandalism which brought the boys to court had been committed in company with other boys. All of the boys were members of either loosely-knit or well-organized street gangs which either had or soon developed "traditions" of group delinquency.

Half of the boys placed in this category had been referred for psychiatric examination because of their behavior. All were found to be without psychosis. Two were without conspicuous mental pathology of any kind and two were "psychoneurotic." Four of the others were quickly found to be characterized by "personality disorders." After several examinations, the last of the nine was also thought to be characterized by a "personality disorder."

Intelligence tests indicated that eight of the boys were functioning at the "average or better" level, nine were "dull and backward," and one was moderately "feebleminded."

The following case material illustrates the kind of vandal placed in this category. It is the case of a gregarious teenager who was on reasonably good terms with his family and socially well adjusted but academically retarded in school. His predatory activities appear to have been largely the result of his participation in the delinquent culture of his neighborhood. Not only does the material describe how boys may sometimes be conscripted as members of well-knit street gangs, but it also shows how, according to Edwin H. Sutherland's theory of "differential association," delinquent behavior may be learned through intimate association with other delinquents.[11] Clearly the boy described learned from his gang associates much about delinquency, including the techniques of "junking,"[12] the activity which led to his court appearance.

The case is also suggestive of forces which contribute to breaking up the gang. In particular, the case points out the disorganizing effect the incarceration of members may have on gang morale. It also shows the consequences the impending marriage or actual marriage of older members may have on gang alliances. The latter, Frederic M. Thrasher concluded, after his classic study of gangs in Chicago, was "the ultimate undoing of most gangs with the exception, perhaps, of the distinctly criminal groups of the professional type."[13]

Case Four: The Recruit

Rudy is a thin, adenoidal, nail-biting teenager who timidly peers out at the world from behind large, thick eyeglasses. When he was about twelve years old, he was "initiated" into the Ellsworth Tims, junior affiliates of a gang of older Irish, German and Jewish boys in his neighborhood. The older boys were known as the Ellsworth Seniors and later, after they had merged with another gang, as the Young Bucks. The Ellsworth Boys, both juniors and seniors, occasionally fought rival gangs, including the Dudes who lived in a nearby Italian neighborhood. On one occasion, some of the older boys, including Rudy's brother, Johnnie, shot and seriously wounded a youth from another group called the Imperial Knights.

In speaking about how he had become a member of the Tims,

---

[11] For the details of this theory, see E. H. Sutherland: *Principles of Criminology*, fourth edition. Chicago, J. B. Lippincott Company, 1947, chap. I.

For a discussion of the role of the gang in teaching the child the techniques of delinquency, as well as a delinquent philosophy of life, see F. M. Thrasher, *The Gang*, second revised edition. Chicago, University of Chicago Press, 1936, chap. XIX.

[12] Gathering metal and other materials to sell for junk is the well documented activity of some gang boys. Sometimes property is destroyed in the process of securing the scrap. In fact, one of the important aspects of junking is the encouragement some junkdealers give children to commit delinquencies to secure scrap. See *ibid.*, chap. IX.

[13] *Ibid.*, p. 242.

Rudy said, "When I was around eleven, we usta hang around there (a street named Ellsworth Place). A bunch of us, I'd say around twelve of us, usta hang around together. We usta fool around with them guys (the Seniors) playin' games and that. We were friends—great friends. They come inta a bigger gang (the Young Bucks) and they wanted us to be like Ellsworth Tims. They grabbed me and another guy and they said that they would 'initiate' us inta a different gang. We didn't know what it was. So they fooled around with us, beat us up and that, like 'initiation,' and we were in the Tims."

Describing where his gang used to "hang out" and their conflict with the police, school personnel and other community representatives, Rudy said, "First it was Ellsworth Place. Then the cops usta chase us from there. Then we'd go someplace else, maybe the school yard. Then we'd get chased from there. Then we'd go to the playground and get chased from there. Wherever ya could stay, ya stayed."

When asked about the fights in which he and his friends had participated, and in particular about the shooting in which the older boys were involved, Rudy said, "Some guys would start in to make themselves a gang. They thought they were 'big.' They would come around and we'd go back after them. When there was a fight, everyone was willin' ta fight. One time, they (the older boys) got in trouble with a shootin'. They weren't called the Ellsworth Boys then. They were called the Young Bucks. They (the Imperial Knights) beat up some guy—one of the guys that usta hang around us—and the guys went back after them. The way I heard it, they weren't goin' ta shoot the guy. They were supposed ta scare him. The gun was 'hair triggered,' that's what I was told, and it went off. It was a 25 (caliber) pistol. The other gang, who my friends were after, said he wasn't one of them, but he *was* one of them,. My brother Johnnie was the one who they (the Knights) beat up. His girl friend lived up towards Prescott Avenue and he walked his girl friend home and them guys grabbed him 'cause they lived in that neighborhood. They beat him up. My friends went back up the following night afterwards. They were looking for any one of them. It didn't matter who it was. They grabbed this guy and they shot him. Some of them went on probation. Some of them got locked up. I think two or three got sent away. The guy who pulled the trigger and the guy who was carryin' the gun to give to the guy who pulled the trigger. They ain't no more gang. Since the shootin' they all broke up. They don't bother with one another. They talk ta one another. I mean they don't hang around in gangs no more. Some of them are gettin' married. They stopped lookin' for fights right after the shootin'. They didn't wanna get in no more trouble. One guy, I think, went inta the army reserve."

Shortly before this shooting occurred, Rudy first became acquainted with Fred, a boy about his own age. Fred later appeared with Rudy in Children's Court after the two of them had climbed to the roof of a school and torn up "copper flashing" which they wanted to sell for junk. For this vandalism, both boys were placed on probation. Rudy said that Fred, although he lived several blocks away, used to "come around once in a while." Gradually the two boys became well acquainted, although Fred was more a fringe member of the Tims than a full-fledged member, even though he sometimes would "help out" in a fight when needed.

The two boys went to court for their first and only appearance when Rudy was fourteen and Fred thirteen. Fred had previously been involved with the police over the theft of brass hand rails which he had taken from an apartment house to sell for junk.

In explaining their vandalism, Rudy said, "We got ta talkin' about it and that was it. Could have been the week before. We just talked about it. We'd say, 'Let's go tomorrow night.' We met that Saturday morning (the day the vandalism was committed), so we said, 'Let's go.'"

Rudy described the manner in which he and Fred had learned to dispose of scrap metal by saying, "Most places won't take it off ya if you're a minor. First ya have ta find a guy whose goin' ta take it off ya. Then, after ya got it, ya can dispose of it right away. Ya find out from other guys where they went and then ya go where they went. Sometimes ya go with them when they sell it. You're 'curious.' Ya wanna find out where they sell it, so ya go with them." Rudy continued by saying that most of the Ellsworth Boys had sold scrap metal for junk and by explaining that "the big ones was the ones that started it."

Speaking of the "zip guns" he and his friends had sometimes made, Rudy said, "We more or less made them just to show we knew how to make them." Then he related the formula[14] for making such a weapon. "Ya get a car antenna and a piece of wood and a can opener. Ya cut out a piece of wood in the design of a gun. Then ya drill a hole (lengthwise) right through the middle on the top and stick ya antenna in there and then ya take ya can opener and take the top off—what ya turn with—then ya file a point on it. Then ya have a hole in the gun and ya stick the can opener top in it. Then ya tie rubber bands on it and pull it back ta fire ya gun."

When asked where he would get an automobile antenna when he had wanted to make a gun, Rudy replied incredulously, "From an automobile on the street. Ya either break it off or twist it off." Asked if he had ever bought an antenna when he needed one, he quite matter-of-factly replied, "Nah—why should ya buy one when they're out on the street ta take? They cost a coupla dollars."

At the time Rudy was taken to court for his vandalism on the school roof, his family had been living in their apartment house, where his mother "supered," for some five years. The building was located in a neighborhood in the central Bronx where the population was predominantly white. For the mother's work, the family received free rent and $65 per month. This supplemented the weekly payments Rudy's father received from Workman's Compensation and the modest salary Rudy's elder sister brought home from her clerical job. The father had been employed as a moving man, but although a comparatively young man, he had suffered a "brain hemorrhage" and was forced to remain idle at home.

The father, a native of New York City, had married Rudy's mother, a rather "warm and intelligent person," who was also born in the city, in a Catholic religious ceremony some four years before Rudy was born. The parents had five children, four boys and a girl. As noted, Johnnie, Rudy's oldest brother, had also been a member of the Ellsworth Boys, as had another brother, Dennis, who was about the same age as Rudy. As far

---

[14] It is interesting to note that numerous boys interviewed during this research could repeat approximately the same "formula" for making a zip gun when asked. Zip gun making appears to be a cultural item shared by a number of boys. It always appears to involve twisting or bending radio antennas from automobiles. Cf., e.g., R. V. McCann: The gift of self: Breaking through to the delinquent. *Religious Education,* 52 (May-June, 1957), pp. 163-168.

as the quality of his intrafamilial relationships was concerned, Rudy said that he "got along well" with both his siblings and his parents. After his court appearance the boy told his probation officer that he was quite disturbed about his involvement with the authorities and the effect it might have on his father's health. Rudy's mother had similarly expressed her concern about the effect her son's delinquency might have on her husband's health.

The parents raised their children in the Catholic faith, and, according to the mother, the family attended church regularly. However, Rudy admitted that he had been "more religious" when attending St. William's Parochial School, which the children in his family traditionally attended, than he had been since graduating from the school, a year after being discharged from probation.

At St. William's Rudy was forced to repeat three grades. Psychological testing indicated that he was an intellectually dull boy. However, he was not a truant nor a behavior problem in the classroom.

When he was in grammar school, Rudy's favorite pastime was ball playing, although he also enjoyed raising and flying pigeons, a popular neighborhood activity. During the winter he used to spend much of his time in neighborhood candy stores. He and his friends also used to "fool around" St. William's Community Center, weight lifting, listening to records, and attending the dances. As far as the parish priests were concerned, Rudy said that, although he knew them, "we never bothered with one another."

The summer Rudy graduated from school he went to work on his uncle's "chicken farm" in upstate New York. That September he returned to New York City and entered Vocational High School with a friend of his from St. William's, about whom Rudy said, "Me and him started in the first grade together. We got left back together. In every class we got left back, we got left back in the same class."

After "three days" at high school Rudy quit. He explained his reasons for leaving by saying, "I didn't like the teachers, so I quit. Loud mouths! Just walk inta a class and they tell ya, 'Sit down! Shut up!' I didn't like it, so I quit." He then went to work in a neighborhood fruit store. Asked if he had been well paid at this job, he said, "Nah—they only give ya a coupla dollars. Ya get twenty-five dollars a week, but the standard pay is forty in New York. But they give ya twenty-five. Ya figure it's a chance ta get out of school, so ya take it."

Later he left the fruit store and returned upstate to live with his uncle where, at sixteen, he helps to feed the chickens and spends much of his time "huntin'." When he gets old enough, Rudy, who has not been involved with the police since his court appearance, said, "I'd like ta get a job in construction like m' brother got. He just started and he gets eighty-four dollars a week."

As in the case just described, the next case is also highly suggestive of the demoralizing effect some neighborhoods have on children.[15] However, unlike the preceding case, the following boy was not a member of a well-knit street gang, but one of a small, unorganized group of youngsters whose exciting and adventurous play brought them into conflict with both property owners and authorities. Nevertheless, both cases underscore the proposition, so succinctly stated by Mays, that in delinquency-prone neighborhoods "delinquency is not so much a symptom of maladjustment as of adjustment to a sub-culture in conflict with the culture of the city as a whole."[16]

In the case that follows, not only does the neighborhood appear to serve as fertile ground for the development of delinquency, but the family itself seems to reinforce the drift toward such behavior, particularly because of the instability and rapacious life philosophy of the parents.

Lastly, the case suggests how some boys may contemplate property destruction as a means for obtaining revenge against those who they believe have wronged them.

Case Five: Life Under the "El"

Frankie's neighborhood, located just south of the central Bronx, is dominated by the Third Avenue elevated line. The

[15] For a discussion of the "spirit" of delinquency areas, particularly for suggestions regarding the general disregard for property rights among delinquents in such areas, see C. R. Shaw and H. D. McKay: *Social Factors in Juvenile Delinquency,* National Commission on Law Observance and Enforcement, Report on the Causes of Crime, Vol. II. Washington, Government Printing Office, 1931, chap. IV.

[16] Mays, *op. cit.,* p. 147.

area is one of the most depressed in the Borough. Its population has shifted from white to a mixture of Negro, white, and Puerto Rican, but mostly Negro. The delinquency rate is high and street gangs are common. The buildings house a mélange of seedy walk-up apartments, store-front churches, the inevitable candy stores and rooming houses, Spanish bodegas, taverns, and light manufacturing plants.

Frankie began his delinquent career soon after his family moved into the area when he was five years old. His delinquencies, mostly peccadillos committed in company with his older brother, Willie, usually involved entry into neighborhood buildings and the destruction of property in the course of play. The two boys were frequently accompanied on their escapades by their older sister, Bunny, and their cousin, Robbie. Robbie had lived since birth in the same ramshackle house into which Frankie's family had moved. The school yard next door to the house is elaborately painted with the names of Robbie and his friends, mostly Negroes, several of whom later became friends of Frankie and his brother.

A typical escapade for the two brothers, their sister, and cousin was the exploration of a nearby "pickle factory" which they first entered to look around and to eat pickles, but where they later threw jars of pickles and bottles of ink around "to smash like hand grenades" in the course of having a "pickle fight." When asked to explain his behavior, Willie said, "We wanted to have some fun." Frankie whimsically added, "Besides, pickles taste good."

Willie explained the relationship he and his brother had with their cousin by saying that when they moved to Third Avenue they had not been "used to" Negroes and, since many of the children in the neighborhood were Negro, they had usually spent their time with their cousin. Almost from the beginning friction existed between the brothers and Robbie, even though the three boys spent much time together roaming around the neighborhood. Later, urged by their families, the boys stopped playing together.

This separation was precipitated by another incident in which the three boys were involved. They entered a garage next door to the house in which they lived and severely damaged an automobile and other property stored there. Both brothers blamed Robbie for this episode, as did their mother. The boys claimed that Robbie was the one who had entered the garage first, that he was the one who had shown Frankie how to "keep chickie" (serve as lookout), and that he was the one who had done the damage.

Two days after this incident, Frankie and his brother, this time unaccompanied by their cousin, entered a neighborhood shop, scattered papers and other articles about the office, and damaged machinery which they had tried to start. The shop owner also reported that they had stolen $150 and carried off a box of automatic pencils.

Willie described this incident by saying, "We was playin' hookey, Friday. Me and my brother went over there. We seen this door. It had a hole in it. So we went down the stairs to see what it was like in there. We went in the office and started messin' everythin' up. So we heard this guy comin'. So Frankie started runnin'. So he say, 'Come on, Willie, somebody's comin'!' I didn't believe him, ya know. I didn't hear nothin'. So this guy starts comin' in. I heard the door open. I ran out of the office—I coulda made it. I slipped up on grease. I still coulda made it, but I said, 'What's the use? They're goin' to catch me anyway.' So I just stopped. I told Frankie to keep goin'. So the guy says, 'There was another little boy with him.' They brought me to my house. So Frankie started comin' up the street. So they looked at him and said, 'That's the kid.' Frankie said, "What happened?" Frankie added to Willie's account, "We didn't break no machines, but we tried to start 'em. The office got messed up a lot. We moved the desks. There was a whole box of pens—lead pencils. We were takin' 'em and (throwing them up in the air) sayin', 'Merry Christmas.' "

Both boys vigorously denied that they had taken any money. They had looked for some, they said, but had not found any to take. They were very hostile toward the shop owner after the incident and Willie, particularly, spoke of his desire to "get revenge" on the owner—whom he described as "a fat Jew"—because the owner had said that they had stolen $150 when they had "just been foolin' around" in the shop. Willie said that if he were "bigger" he would "beat up" the owner, but since he was not, he would like to put nails under the "nice tires" of his automobile or smash his windows.

Frankie and his brother were arrested for entering the shop and brought to Children's Court. At the time, Frankie was eight and Willie was eleven. Robbie, their cousin, who was twelve, was taken to court for damaging the automobile. This was the first time the boys had appeared in court. Willie was placed on probation and both Frankie and Robbie were found delinquent and discharged with a warning. Later, Frankie and Willie were taken into the Big Brother program.

Bunny, Frankie and Willie's sister, a sexually precocious child and a runaway, was committed to a state training school a few months before the boys appeared in court. At the time she was thirteen years old.

When asked to explain his delinquencies, Frankie, a pleasant, mild-mannered youngster of high average intelligence who verbalizes and relates easily, said that he and his brother were never "in trouble" before moving to Third Avenue, although there had been ample opportunity for breaking into places where they had previously lived. Frankie continued by saying, "But when ya live here ya see a lotta guys—big guys—doin' that and doin' this and then ya get the habit of it. All the guys where I usta live were 'nice.' The guys around here, they don't do nothin' right. They rob things." To this Willie added, "They do that right out on the street in broad daylight. A mother sends a guy down to get the papers. He picks 'em up, puts 'em under his arm, and walks away. Doesn't even pay for them. One time I was walkin' down Third Avenue—this guy (one of a group of Negro boys) come over to me and say, 'Gimme all the money ya got or I'll kick ya!' So I says, 'You gotta try to take my money.' So they all gang up on me at once. So my father come runnin' across the street. That's when most of them started runnin'. One guy—he was real greedy—he stayed there fightin' me. My father just stood there and watched—to see what I was gonna do, ya know. So the guy had my wallet. He took it out of my pocket. He started runnin'. So I ran over and tripped him, ya know. Like playin' football, but I didn't get hurt. He was the one who got hurt 'cause it was on cement. So I started beatin' him up and everythin'. My father said, 'Hold it! He had enough.' So my father started cursin' him out and everythin'. I still had my money."

Asked if they belonged to the Warriors, the Warrior Tops, or any of the other "clubs" in their neighborhood, first Frankie and then Willie, after explaining that the members of these gangs were "all big guys," said that they did not belong because "ya get in trouble—too much trouble." As far as their cousin Robbie was concerned, he did not belong either because "he can't fight anyway."

Both boys fancifully told as tales of derring-do the experiences their father had as a youth in their present neighborhood, outwitting the police and exerting his physical prowess over his peers. They also enthusiastically described a fight their grandfather once had with a detective in a barroom. The children took special delight in telling how Willie once fooled a supermarket clerk into twice giving them change for the same $20 bill, and how, on one of their trips to Coney Island, they reached into an empty change booth in a subway station and took money and tokens. Asked what his mother would have said had she known about the incident involving the $20 bill, Willie replied, "She probably would have asked me for a coupla dollars."

When asked what he would like to be when he grew up, Frankie wistfully replied that, among other things, he would like to be a fireman because "ya get $200 every two weeks." Willie said that he would like to be "a cop just like Phil Smith." He continued, "He's a cop at the 156th Precinct. He usta come up my house and play cards a lot when he was on duty and every hour he used our phone to call in." Neither boy would like to be like his father " 'cause he drinks a lot."

Frankie's family has been well known to welfare agencies, including the Family Division of the Domestic Relations Court, the Department of Welfare Children's Placement Service, and the Society for Seamen's Children. The contacts began when Frankie was an infant and his mother left the home because of her husband's excessive drinking and physical abuse. She soon returned, but discord continued and the mother left again after the family had been evicted for non-payment of rent. On that occasion, Frankie, his brother and sister were placed in a series of foster homes. Two years later, when Frankie was five years old, the family reunited and moved to Third Avenue.

Both the mother and father were born in the Bronx, as were their children. The parents spent their childhood in the same neighborhood in which the family now lives. The mother, an attractive woman with an engaging personality, graduated from a Bronx junior high school, and the father attended vocational high school. The father is usually employed as a combination truck driver-carpenter-handyman for a refrigeration and fixture concern. Because of a back injury he had received on the job, he was not working when his sons were adjudged delinquent. Referring to this injury, Willie said of his father, "He's supposed to get a settlement—about $5,000 or $6,000. He's waited three or four years already, but he didn't get the settlement yet. My father says he don't care. The longer he waits, the more he's gonna get."

Both parents are Protestant and, at the time the boys went to court, both children were members of a church congregation.

The mother had previously been married at eighteen and divorced. Before her divorce took place, she started living with the man who is her present husband. Their daughter, Bunny, was born before their marriage took place. Willie and Frankie are also children of the mother and her present husband.

Frankie, Willie, and their cousin, Robbie, have not been in serious difficulty with the police since they went to court. However, about a year after their court appearance, a complaint was made against all three boys by a neighbor after they had "accidentally" broken a window in his car with a stone.

At the present time, Frankie, at the age of eleven, is in the fifth grade at the public school on Third Avenue next door to where he lives. Although his general academic adjustment has been fairly satisfactory, he was recently placed in an "opportunity class" because of his reading retardation. His social adjustment in school has also been satisfactory, although the pattern of truancy, which started before his court appearance, continues.

Most students of the gang suggest that such groups are primarily, but not exclusively, found in "interstitial" urban areas and among working-class people.[17] The following case illustrates the delinquent gang as it may be found in relatively stable neighborhoods among "middle-class" boys.

The superiority of the gang over the family, church, and school in influencing the behavior of its members is most apparent in the life history of the central figure in this case. Although well adjusted at home, active in his church, and, until he became fully incorporated into his gang, a boy who was making a satisfactory

---

[17] See, e.g., A. K. Cohen: *Delinquent Boys: The Culture of the Gang.* Glencoe, Illinois, The Free Press, 1955, pp. 36-44; Thrasher, *op. cit.*, chap. I.

adaptation to school, this youth continued his rebellious group delinquencies until he left the gang, renewed his association with his non-delinquent friends, and became gainfully employed.

Particularly noticeable in this case was the inability of one community agency—the authorities in the private housing development which served as the gang locale—to regulate the behavior of this group. In fact, conflict with these authorities, which continued until the gang transferred its activities elsewhere after some of its members and their families had been "encouraged" to move, appears to have been one of the chief factors which contributed to the development of gang morale and solidarity. The case also shows how physical prowess, "just plain orneriness," and the property destruction which the community frequently brands as "senseless," can enhance the personal reputations of individual gang boys. The case indicates, as well, that members of such gangs may in fact take pride in the rambunctious behavior and sheer "toughness" of their groups.

Finally, the material shows that even marauding youths of this type may refrain from destroying some categories of property—in this case property belonging to their own church which they "respected." Moreover, boys like these who are likely to have reputations as "cop haters" may realistically distinguish between private police of the custodian type and regular law-enforcement officers who are armed and backed by the authority of the state. While the former may be treated with derision and as objects of harassment, the latter are avoided whenever possible. However, it is interesting to note that in a time of crisis, true to their tradition of toughness and in keeping with the high potential for violence generally characteristic of belligerent youth gangs, members of the group described did not hesitate to assault a city police officer who had interrupted one of their soirees and arrested their leader.

Case Six: A "Middle-Class" Hooligan

Hugh and his friends were members of the Manhattan Avenue Boys. This gang was a closely-knit group of thirty or more Irish, German, and Italian boys that made its headquarters in Bronxchester, an all-white, middle-class housing development in the east Bronx. The fathers of the boys were policemen, firemen, or were otherwise employed by municipal departments. Some worked as telephone installers, garage foremen, or office clerks. Hugh lived a short distance away from Bronxchester in an almost exclusively white neighborhood in one of the better areas of the Bronx. Carl, Hugh's best friend, and most of the other members of the Manhattans lived in the Bronxchester development. During the time he belonged to the Manhattans, Hugh "never bothered with" boys in his own neighborhood, but preferred the company of his Bronxchester friends, most of whom had attended Saint Patrick's school with him. As Hugh phrased it, "I usta like the guys in Bronxchester. I was havin' a good time and everything—a lot of fun." When not in school, the boys used to spend their time in and about Bronxchester sitting on the park benches or in a nearby candy store. They also played cards, "made out with the girls"—sometimes called the Manhattan Debs—spent time "drinkin' up some guy's apartment," or attending dances and sodality meetings run by the local parish.

Although Bronxchester is located in an area which officially has an extremely low delinquency rate, the Manhattans were in constant conflict with the housing development police, with the residents of the area, and sometimes with other gangs in the Bronx. Occasionally they "used to go down to 149th Street and fight the Spics down there." According to one resident of the area, they also "used to go into the (nearby) movie, parade up and down the center aisle in front of all the people yelling, 'We're the Manhattans!' A couple even went up on the stage and tried to rip the curtain down. They were very proud of their gang." The files which the Bronxchester authorities keep on all troublesome children living in the development show that Carl, Hugh's friend, had been reprimanded by them on over twenty occasions, mostly for disorderly conduct, bullying other children, fighting in company with his friends, and sometimes for destroying property. Most of these disturbances occurred after Carl—a youth who frequently sauntered about Bronxchester accompanied by his "lieutenants"—had assumed informal leadership of the Manhattans. The disturbances culminated in an incident for which Hugh and Carl were arrested and adjudged delinquent when both were fifteen years old.

Hugh described the incident, which involved vandalism and

an attack upon a New York City police lieutenant, in these words, "We went down to this bar. Guess there was just four of us there and we stayed there for a while. We were drunk, I guess. We ran out of money. We left and we said we were gonna see if we met anybody walkin' through Bronxchester and we were gonna beat them up and rob them, ya know, so that we could have more money to go back. Also we were gonna go 'beat up' a Bronxchester cop. We walked all the way through Bronxchester. Thank goodness we didn't meet anybody while walkin' through. And we walked over to Bronx Avenue by Westford there. And that's where we were makin' a lot of noise and everything. Jumped on a few cars and broke a few windows, I guess. Then this cop came along and said he was gonna arrest us and we said, 'No you're not!' By then we had met a few more friends over there. I guess there was about eight of us now. And he grabbed us and we broke loose and he held onto Carl and said he was gonna take him in and we said, 'No,' and he started fightin' with Carl 'cause Carl didn't want to go. He ripped his shirt and then Carl got mad and we all started walkin' toward him and he pulled his gun. And we just kept walkin' and he went to shoot and, I guess, Carl hit his hand and the shot went into the buildin' or something'. So then him and Carl fell between two cars. We saw more cops were comin' so we took off. We cut through a buildin' and a cop chased us through there. We ran out another buildin' and there was a carload of Bronxchester cops. They called us, but we kept goin'. Then I ran into a cop down by the baseball field and he grabbed me and brought me back."

As the result of this delinquency, both Hugh and Carl, neither of whom had previously appeared in Children's Court, were placed on probation. Hugh never again appeared before Children's Court, but some four months after the attack on the police lieutenant, Carl was again brought to the same court, this time for auto theft in company with some friends.

Explaining the conflict he and his friends had with the housing development police, Hugh, who referred frequently to his gang as having been the "toughest" in its neighborhood, said that a few nights before the delinquency for which he went to court, he and some of his friends were "breaking this cop's horns" (annoying a Bronxchester policeman) as part of the long-continued antagonism existing between the Manhattans and the development police. He continued by saying that the Bronxchester police "didn't like us. They wouldn't let us hang out any place. They kept chasin' us. There was a few nice guys and lot of them who weren't. Like they would wait to catch us one at a time or somethin' like that with two or three of them. And they would try to do somethin' to us. Like they grabbed this Carl one time and they said if we kept beatin' their cops up and everything, they were gonna put Carl in the hospital. So he told them, 'For every one of us you put in the hospital, we're gonna put three of you in the hospital.' "

Of the relationships the Manhattans had with the development police, Hugh also said that he and his friends "didn't care. They wouldn't do nothin' to us. Actually they were afraid of us." However, he pointed out that his group usually avoided difficulty with the New York City police who, unlike the housing development police, "had guns and night sticks."

Hugh is a tall, heavy-set youth of high average intelligence, but although direct and forceful in manner, he is not a leader. He first met Carl when they both attended parochial grammar school and they remained friends until they both appeared in court when Hugh was told to stay out of Bronxchester "for five years." After that, Hugh left the Manhattans and renewed his friendships with the somewhat older, non-delinquent youths in his neighborhood. Many of these young men were married.

Meanwhile, Carl's family and the families of some of the other Manhattans had been prevailed upon by the management of the housing development to move elsewhere. Thereafter, according to one of the development officials, the gang no longer frequented Bronxchester, although more than a year after the affair with the police lieutenant, Carl and some of his friends and their girl friends, but not including Hugh, were apprehended in a "club" they had taken over in an apartment house adjacent to Bronxchester, after neighbors had called the police because of the noise, beer drinking, and revelry of the group.

Observers of the Manhattans report that the gang started in the housing development some six or seven years before Hugh and Carl appeared in court and that Carl was the third boy who had served as the informal leader of the group. According to Hugh, these older youths had gone into military service by the time he had become friendly with Carl and the younger boys. According to residents of the area, the leader before Carl "would do anything for a laugh," especially destroying property or starting fights with strangers in front of his friends. This youth "had a great deal of influence on the other gangs around there because of his reputation as being more or less of a 'nut' who would do anything. A lot of fellas were afraid of him. He would think nothing of pulling out a knife at the drop of a hat —threatening somebody or cutting up the seats in the 'Royal' movie." The Manhattans "were as much afraid of him as other people were."

Asked about some property destruction at Saint Patrick's school in which the Manhattans were believed to have been implicated, Hugh insisted that his friends would never destroy Church property because, as he put it, "We respect it." However, he did admit that they "might do somethin' to a Protestant church," and at one time they had caused a disturbance at a synagogue.

Hugh was born in New York City as were both his parents. The mother, herself a direct and forceful Irish woman, who was definitely "the head of the family," married Hugh's father in a Catholic religious ceremony some four years before Hugh was born. Hugh is one of two children. His older brother, who was in the army at the time Hugh appeared in court, had himself been brought to Children's Court after threatening a salesman with a knife. At the time Hugh appeared in court the family regularly attended their parish church. Hugh's father, who usually worked as an auditor, had been unemployed for several months before Hugh went to court. The father had previously been steadily employed for years, but the firm he had worked for had gone out of business and he had had difficulty in finding work because of his age and because of an accident that temporarily incapacitated him. At the time Hugh was brought to court, his mother was working as a bookkeeper at a salary of eighty dollars per week.

In talking with Hugh's probation officer, the mother said that she could offer no explanation for her son's delinquency, although she believed he had gotten into difficulty because of his friends. She said, too, that the four members of the family had good relationships with each other, although there had been some difficulties since her husband lost his job and because of the medical expenses incurred by his recent injury. The mother told the probation officer that Hugh's conduct at home had been good and that until he had been arrested she had been unaware of his outside activities. She said she had felt his behavior outside the home had been satisfactory as he had regularly participated in parish social activities with his friends. Later, the mother said that Hugh had seemed to think that Carl was a "big shot. He looked up to him. He thought that Carl could do anything." She also related how "helpless" she had felt in court when she had appeared with Hugh. She said, "They settled the whole thing without us. We might just as well not have been there. Nothing I said seemed to matter. I had hired a lawyer, but he was worthless. He didn't get a chance to say anything."

At the parish school which he had attended, Hugh had not been a truant and his academic adjustment had been good. His conduct grades were "A." However, his academic adjustment deteriorated soon after he entered Central Catholic High School about the time he had become actively involved with the Manhattans, which was some two years before he participated in the assault on the police lieutenant. After a year at Central, where he had played both football and "hookey," he had been asked to leave. He transferred to a public high school for a short time. After that, according to Hugh, who was not attending any school at the time he appeared in court, "I got a note from a doctor saying that I couldn't go to school, so I didn't go to school at all. So then they started troublin' me about 'continuation school,' ya know, once a week. So I went there about three times or twice. I didn't like it. There was too many Spics in the school and too many niggers. I didn't care for that, so I never went."

Shortly after the incident with the police lieutenant, Hugh, at sixteen, took a job in construction work for which he is especially suited because of his physique. At the age of eighteen, he is working as a "steel carrier" for another construction company earning $3.15 an hour, plus $4.97 an hour overtime. He is looking forward to getting a better job paying $4.00 an hour with the same construction company. He continues to live at home and gives his mother some fifty dollars per week. Recently he helped to pay for the summer "bungalow" his family took at Rockaway Beach. On weekends, he drives his new Dodge convertible on dates with several different girls, plays football with a team from Throggs Neck, and drinks beer with a "college crowd"—which Hugh describes as "all clean cut lookin' guys"—around a juke box in a nearby tavern. About "cops" Hugh says, "I don't like them or anybody like them. I wouldn't have anything to do with them if I could help it."

After appraising the results of ecological studies of delinquency in twenty American cities, Shaw and McKay said:

> Year after year, decade after decade, large cities—and especially certain areas in large cities—send to the courts an undiminished line of juvenile offenders. Year after year, decade after decade, likewise, society continues to organize or construct new agencies or institutions designed to reduce the number of these offenders and to rehabilitate those who have already offended against the law. Perhaps the unsatisfactory results of these treatment and prevention efforts have been due, in part at least, to the fact that our attention has been focused too much upon the individual delinquent and not enough upon the setting in which delinquency arises.[18]

Granting the validity of this observation, much is amiss in our efforts to prevent juvenile delinquency by "treating" individual offenders, while ignoring the realities of their life situations.

The last case to be presented in this chapter is suggestive of the difficulties faced by courts and correctional institutions when they attempt to rehabilitate offenders coming from delinquency-prone neighborhoods without being able to alter the demoralizing milieu in which such offenders live and to which they respond. Twice the teenager in the following case was placed on probation and twice he was again almost immediately involved in delinquency, each time in company with his peers and in situations arising out of his neighborhood milieu. One can only guess what the eventual adjustment of this youth will be when he leaves the correctional institution in which he is presently confined. However, it is perhaps significantly ominous that he has been denied parole and must serve his maximum sentence.

In addition, the following case, as well as the others presented

[18] C. R. Shaw and H. D. McKay: *Juvenile Delinquency and Urban Areas.* Chicago, University of Chicago Press, 1942, p. 446. (Reprinted by permission.)

in this section, shows how property destruction is only one aspect of the delinquent activities of most of the boys classified as Subcultural Vandals. Such boys are not merely vandals, and this is an important point, but are boys who have been engaged in a variety of delinquent behavior over an extended period of time, as have the Disturbed Vandals considered earlier.

Lastly, the material indicates the role parent-child tensions and rivalries may play in alienating boys of this type from their homes, thereby placing them in position to be easily influenced by neighborhood cultures.

Case Seven: Prognosis "Guarded"

Leroy, the father of a three-year-old daughter, is a tall, athletic, nineteen-year-old, southern-born Negro presently serving a three-year sentence in a state correctional institution. He was sentenced for the crime of "rape as a misdemeanor" by the Bronx County Court after he and another youth had had sexual intercourse with the fourteen-year-old sister of one of Leroy's former girl friends.

When asked about the offense which led to his imprisonment at the age of seventeen, Leroy said, "It never occurred to me that I wuz breakin' the law. I had intercourses before. This girl didn't protest or nothin'. As a matter of fact, she dared me to do it. We took her up on the roof and Melvin started first on the roof landin'. Afta he finished, I *tried* but cudn't get it in. We went two more roofs down (the block) and then that's where I did it."

The institutional staff has "certified" Leroy as suitable for parole, but the state parole board voted not to parole him after he had appeared before it on three occasions, and to hold him until the expiration of his sentence.

At the state reception center where Leroy was given an intensive diagnostic examination prior to his transfer to his present institution, he was found to be a youth who had had some early religious training, but who had seldom attended church prior to commitment. He was also noted to be a teenager who had recently spent his time on the streets and drinking with his friends. He impressed the reception center staff as being a good sportsman, but a follower who was content to go along with the crowd. In the reception center school he was quiet, attentive, and unusually well mannered. Psychological examination indicated that he was of average intelligence, perhaps higher. On psychiatric examination he did not leave the impression of viciousness, but of a youth who was easily led and influenced. The psychiatric diagnosis rendered was "Behavior Disorder"—prognosis "Guarded."

Later, when Leroy was examined by the psychiatrist at the institution where he is presently confined, he was found to be without psychosis, but a youth who was likely to be motivated by primitive urges and who showed little empathy or consideration for others. He was also noted to have low moral and ethical values.

At first, Leroy made an exceptionally good institutional adjustment. Later, however, just before he appeared before the parole board for the last time, he received three disciplinary reports. One was for "fighting" with another inmate. The second was for having pencils and other "contraband" from the institutional storeroom where he was working at the time. Four other inmates who also worked in the storeroom were also involved in this second report. Leroy received his third report after he and the four inmates who had been involved with him in the second report broke open four bags of flour and threw the contents around the storeroom. Both the second and third reports were made out by the same storeroom employee. One interpretation offered for the storeroom incident at the institution is that both the scattering of the flour and the report itself resulted from the antagonism existing between the inmates involved and the employee, who had previously placed Leroy and the four others on report for possessing contraband.

At one time or another Leroy has been assigned to the "garden squad," to the hospital where he was "first boy," and to the storeroom detail at the institution where he is presently confined. He now attends school in the morning and works in the laundry in the afternoon.

At the time of his arrest for "rape," Leroy was under the supervision of a Bronx County Court probation officer. This court had placed him under supervision soon after his sixteenth birthday and after Leroy and three of his friends had burglarized a Bronx bakery office. This burglary was committed while Leroy was on probation at the Children's Court for vandalism he had committed while still a juvenile.

Leroy, who is quite articulate, described his burglary in these words, "The way it started off there wuz two brothers—one named Billy Simpson and his brother Freddie. Freddie wuz in the service. I wuz supposed to report to Children's Court that day and I let them talk me into going up their house. There wuz more boys there. We wuz playin' records and drinkin' beer and Freddie showed one boy where he kept his money. Freddie walked out of the apartment and came back later on sayin' that twenty dollars of his money wuz gone. Actually nobody left the room (to go) into the other room where he kept his money. That night three boys—they wuz 'hard rocks'—came to get me up my girl friend's house. They took me back to Saxon Avenue. I wuzn't arguin' the point! They started beatin' on me. When I asked why, they told me I already knew. When they saw that I didn't know what they wuz talkin' about, then they told me. I told 'em I didn't have no twenty dollars and I didn't take it. I found out later the other boys (who had been in the apartment) had gone through the same thing. So the three of them told me I had to get up twenty dollars or else pay the consequences. So me and three other boys (who had been in the apartment) went out the next night and I saw the place there—I saw it wuz an office. We got into the place by means of an air conditioner in the winda. I just raised the winda up. We stole two typewriters, and an adding machine, and other office things. We found some checks and they spread 'em all over the room. We walked up to Crotona Park and that's where the police officer caught us."

A month before he was arrested for this burglary, Leroy, an older youth named Bobby, and three younger friends (who were not apprehended) had tried to smash open a parking meter with a hatchet. This was the vandalism for which Leroy was taken to Children's Court and placed on probation.

When asked about the parking meter incident, Leroy said that Bobby had suggested that they break open parking meters for the coins inside. Leroy further explained that he had never had any money of his own; that any time he had wanted a quarter or a dime he had had to ask his mother or step-father, whom he disliked, for it; and that he thought it would "feel good" to have some money. Leroy described the incident itself in the following manner, "We started off—me and Bobby and the rest of the boys wuz discussin' it. So after we discussed it, we decided to go through with it. We went and started to break open this parkin' meter with a hatchet, but we didn't get into it 'cause we wuz 'interrupted' by the police. Then they took us down the station and Bobby spent the night and my parents came for me."

Asked if he and his friends were a "gang," Leroy answered, "We wuzn't a gang 'cause we didn't go around molestin' nobody." However, he said that these boys were well known to him as they were among the twenty or so Negro, Irish, and Italian boys with whom he had spent his time when he lived in the Bronx. He added that several of these boys, besides himself, had been "sent away" for one reason or another.

Questioned about other delinquencies, Leroy insisted that he had only been in difficulty with the police on three occasions. He vaguely recalled, however, that on one of his summer vacations down south, before he had been brought to Children's Court, he had been chased by a man with a gun after he and some other boys had gone into a building and he had used the telephone to call New York.

Leroy, an only child, was born in a small town in North Carolina, while his mother, a woman with a grammar school education, was married to her first husband. When Leroy was about one year old, his mother took him to New York City where she came to live after divorcing his father. The mother married again when her son was ten years old. Although she is not Roman Catholic, her second husband is, and their marriage took place at a parish church in the Bronx. Leroy's step-father, a man several years younger than his wife, and with a business school education, usually works as a post office clerk. However, at the time Leroy appeared in Children's Court the step-father was unemployed because of an injury he had received at work . Leroy's mother works as a machine operator in the New York fabric industry. At the time Leroy committed his vandalism, he, his mother, and his step-father had lived for six years in an apartment in the south Bronx. The neighborhood is one of the most depressed in the borough and has a moderately high delinquency rate. Many of the buildings are being torn down to make room for a new housing development. The area, although mostly white, has many Negroes and contains one of the heaviest concentrations of Puerto Ricans in the borough. Leroy's mother and step-father lived in three rooms of a six-room apartment,

Leroy slept in the apartment of his maternal grandmother in the same building.

Leroy's Children's Court probation officer noted that there appeared to be conflict between the grandmother and the step-father over supervision of the boy, as well as competition between the boy and his step-father over the mother's attention. To the probation officer, Leroy seemed to be much more closely associated with an uncle, his mother's brother, than with his step-father. When interviewed at Children's Court, Leroy's step-father described his marriage as a "good" one, but said that Leroy was "lazy, indifferent in the home," and refused to "obey anyone." Both parents said that the boy had been associating with "undesirables in the community" and that he refused "to keep good hours." Later, Leroy himself described his relationship with his mother as "very good," but said his relationship with his step-father was "not too good." The Children's Court probation officer also reported that Leroy spent much time playing with his friends in the parks, on the street, and at the local community center. At one time, the report continues, Leroy and his friends "hooked up" their own basketball court so that they could practice for their games with other teams at the community center. The probation officer further noted that the step-father also played basketball, had met Leroy in competition and had boasted to the boy about his superior ability at this sport. To this, the officer reported, Leroy responded with resentment.

Leroy entered public school in the Bronx when he was six years old. In the last grade of grammar school he had a low "C" average and his social adjustment was unsatisfactory. By the time he entered vocational high school at thirteen he had become a truant and his academic adjustment was very poor. A teacher at the high school described Leroy as a boy "who could get by," but who "just didn't give a damn." Leroy obtained working papers a few months after he committed his burglary, and left high school. Shortly thereafter he was arrested for his most recent offense.

Leroy was converted to Catholicism when he was thirteen years old. He explained this by saying that he had become a Catholic because many of the friends he had had at that time were Catholics, as was a woman he liked very much who lived downstairs in his apartment house. He indicated that he had also liked the general atmosphere in the parish church; that he had enjoyed going there to pray; and that he had been friends with one of the parish priests who had even come to see him after he had first been in trouble. However, he admits that in recent years he has been indifferent about church.

About the future Leroy is indefinite. At one time, he said that he had thought he might marry the girl who is the mother of his daughter. He said that this girl, who is somewhat older than he is, even now regularly brought the child to visit his mother and step-father. However, he concluded that since he now knows that any such plans will not help him to be paroled, he is not much interested in going through with such a marriage, especially since the girl now has another out-of-wedlock child and is pregnant with her third. Most of all, Leroy indicated, he would prefer to live down south with his father, whom he used to visit on summer vacations. He also said that he liked the boys down south better than the ones he had known in New York.

Chapter IV

TYPES OF VANDALISM

It is commonly assumed that human behavior is not aimless activity but is motivated behavior directed at the achievement of some end or goal. In essence, human behavior is purposeful and meaningful behavior.

But for the social scientist the study of human behavior involves more than just the study of motivation. As the social psychologist W. I. Thomas put it, human behavior occurs only under conditions called "situations" and it is the task of social science to study human situations in terms of both their "objective" and "subjective" aspects. Objective aspects of situations are factors in the situation "common to both the observer and the actor, such as physical environment, relevant social norms, and the behavior of others." Subjective factors are "factors that exist only for the actors, i.e., how they perceive the situation, what it means to them, what their 'definition' of the situation is."[1]

According to this view, then, human behavior "cannot be understood apart from the situation in which it occurs and to which it is a potential adjustment."[2] Thus, for the social scientist studying human behavior, the crucial concepts are those of "situation" and the "definition of the situation" held by actors attempting to solve particular problems or to achieve special goals through concrete activity in specific situations.

The purpose of this chapter is two-fold: (1) to suggest a general descriptive typology of vandalism derived from an analy-

[1] E. H. Volkart (ed.): *Social Behavior and Personality: Contributions of W. I. Thomas to Theory and Social Research.* New York, Social Science Research Council, 1951, p. 2.

[2] *Ibid.*, p. 6.

sis of both the "objective" and "subjective" aspects of the situations in which such destruction occurs; (2) to use this typology to classify the particular incidents of vandalism which brought the delinquents described in Chapter III before the Bronx Children's Court.

A GENERAL TYPOLOGY OF VANDALISM

Perusal of assorted incidents of vandalism reported in the daily press, described in various kinds of case material available in the literature, as well as material from other sources, suggested that vandalism could be divided into three basic but sometimes overlapping subtypes: *Predatory Vandalism, Vindictive Vandalism,* and *Wanton Vandalism.*[3]

Predatory Vandalism

Albert K. Cohen has drawn attention to the fact that many students have noted the "non-utilitarian" aspects of delinquent behavior, particularly the non-materialistic motivations in juvenile theft.[4] The important point here is that, while much adult crime is economically motivated, juvenile theft occurs as much "for fun" or "sport" as for material gain. However, this does not deny the possibility, or even the likelihood, that the rational desire for "scarce goods" may play a predominant, if not an exclusive, part in the delinquency of some children. Acknowledging this possibility, Tappan, one of those who have written of the non-materialistic aspects of juvenile theft,[5] cites the following case.

> Jack Harash, a boy of fourteen, was discovered on the roof of a closed theater in the act of ripping off copper drains with a meathook. It was an old theater and groups of boys had re-

---

[3] It must be noted that a residual category of vandalism consisting of a miscellany of acts not classifiable by this typology also appears to exist. This category includes, for example, breaking windows for the purpose of "displaying one's masculinity," certain kinds of "tactical" vandalism, such as is sometimes committed by sailors who damage their ships to delay their return to sea, and the "accidental" but nonetheless culpable destruction of property.

[4] A. K. Cohen: *Delinquent Boys: The Culture of the Gang.* Glencoe, Illinois, The Free Press, 1955, p. 184.

[5] P. W. Tappan: *Juvenile Delinquency.* New York, McGraw-Hill Book Company, 1949, p. 143.

peatedly taken turns at ripping up the flashings. The boy explained that four months before, he and his brother had found some copper and sold it to the men "who stand around in front of the junk shops and sell the copper for us, because children aren't allowed to sell it. Since then we have been looking for it whenever we could. We give the money to our mother. She thinks we find the stuff in lots. She doesn't know we go into buildings." The probation officer found the father had been out of work and that the boys had supplemented the meager family income in this way and by delivering papers. The regular family income consisted of $5 from one sister $10 from another.[6]

While Thrasher has drawn attention to "the sport motive" in juvenile theft,[7] he has also written of the economic rewards, "junking," often involving property destruction and theft, can have for gang boys. Among others, he cites the following case.

Anthony, a fifteen-year-old youngster, with three companions, broke into an empty house. In cutting out the lead pipe, they did $200 damage, but the junk-peddler who purchased the loot gave the boys only $1.50 each. The dealer was afterward arrested for receiving stolen property. This gang also robbed freight cars. . . .[8]

Life history material by one of the Martin brothers, well known to readers of the delinquency monographs written by members of the "Chicago School" of sociology, further illustrates "junking" as a form of "predatory" destruction. Despite its illegality, the vandalism described in the following document appears to have been essentially economic activity reflecting the competitive "spirit" of the American business ethic.

I guess that I took part in all the trivial, mischievous things that a small boy does who isn't brought up in the proper manner. One of my playful habits when I was short of a little ready cash

---

[6] From J. W. Polier: *Everyone's Children, Nobody's Child.* New York, Charles Scribner's Sons, 1941, as cited by Tappan, *op. cit.*, p. 145. (Reprinted by permission.)

[7] F. M. Thrasher: *The Gang,* second revised edition. Chicago, University of Chicago Press, 1936, p. 92.

[8] *Ibid.*, p. 150.

> was to go junking. Only the junking that I did wasn't exactly within the law. To me, however, nothing was outside the law. Whatever I did I never thought twice of whether it was right or wrong in the average person's eyes. The junking that I'm referring to was fairly lucrative. It was procuring lead. . . . There are only two places where lead is found. One is in the earth. The other is in old, abandoned houses. But I didn't go to the mines in Montana for my mineral. That would require too much effort, and think of the distance that I'd have to cover. Besides, I'd have to pay freight charges if I did that, so it wouldn't be worth the trouble. Instead of going to all that trouble I decided to remain in Chicago and get a corner on the lead market here. As there was a plentiful supply here, I decided it was the best thing to do. Other kids in the neighborhood did the same thing.
>
> Whenever I felt the urge I'd go walking through the neighborhood until I'd see some old, empty shack that looked as if it was ready to fall over. Sometimes I went alone; other times kids from my gang went with me. As a rule there were always lead pipes in these old buildings, but at times I was too late as some other vandal—or shall I say competitor—had beaten me to it. However when I did go into a house and there was any lead in it, why, I'd help myself. Usually, I would only take it out of the cellar, but as competition grew stronger I would have to climb up to the first and second floors for my lead as the lead in the cellar would be gone. Even the houses in good order didn't escape my tour of inspection.
>
> Even though they were empty but were ready for occupancy I would force my way into them and take all the lead I could carry. . . .[9]

Other facets of "predatory" property destruction are suggested by the following incidents of vandalism reported in the daily press. The first tells of telephone cable theft near Detroit, Michigan, while the second describes the smashing and looting of parking meters in Massachusetts.

---

[9] C. R. Shaw (ed.): *Brothers in Crime.* Chicago, University of Chicago Press, 1938; Philadelphia, A. Saifer, 1952, pp. 156-157. (Reprinted by permission.)

Cable Thieves Cut Off Detroit

DETROIT, Aug. 25 (AP)—Thieves took 500 feet of heavy cable last night from the American Telephone and Telegraph Company's trunk line between Detroit and Toledo. They apparently used a truck to carry the cable away. The break temporarily cut off all Detroit communications to the South and East.[10]

Parking Meters Looted

Twenty parking meters were smashed and looted Saturday night within a 250-yard radius of Union, Foster and North Foster Streets.

Police said they could not estimate how much money was contained in the stolen meter coin boxes.

Twelve of the smashed meters were on Union Street near Exchange. Six were on Foster Street and two more on North Foster.[11]

Two interesting variations of Predatory Vandalism were reported by R. R. Prewer in his assessment of a group of adult window-smashers in Great Britain.[12] The first refers to the custom, apparently common among some vagrants and other homeless wanderers, of smashing windows or committing other minor offenses for the purpose of securing a warm bed and good food in a police station or prison. Prewer noted that among the prisoners he examined quite a few "regulars" worked this sort of stratagem, especially toward the approach of the Christmas season. Far from being deterred, individuals of this kind are encouraged to repeat by the very benefits they derive from imprisonment.

---

[10] *The New York Times,* August 26, 1955.

[11] *Worcester* (Massachusetts) *Telegram,* December 30, 1957.

An indication of the extensive loss some cities suffer from the looting of parking meters is provided by a news item in the *Chicago Daily News,* December 27, 1958. This report stated that more than 20,000 of Chicago's 30,000 parking meters were looted by vandals in 1958 and that the lost revenue alone amounted to about $2,000 a week, or about $100,000 for the year.

[12] R. R. Prewer: Some observations on window-smashing. *The British Journal of Delinquency,* 10 (October, 1959), pp. 104-113.

The second variation described by Prewer refers to window-smashing as a prelude to theft, as in a "smash-and-grab" raid on the windows of a shop or store. A good example of window breaking for this purpose is found in the following news report.

PANE BREAKER ADMITS NEW $200 CRACKUP

Charles C——, the disbarred lawyer who has been breaking plate-glass windows for the last 22 years to get food or liquor, made his 41st court appearance today and pleaded guilty to smashing a $200 window at 332 Broadway. . . .

The proceedings were brief. C——, who is 65 and has a record of 38 convictions since 1937, had no chance to explain what compels him to break windows to get at food and drink. (Once in a moment of aberration, he took three dummy bottles of milk and was furious and ashamed.) . . .[13]

Vindictive Vandalism

In some vandalism the chief motivation appears to be the desire of the participants to express the antagonism and hatred they feel toward special individuals and groups. Sometimes such animosity seems to be combined with an effort to intimidate particular victims.

Vandalism arising from animosity is clearly illustrated in the following incidents.

PORTRAIT OF IKE SLASHED IN CLUB

HOUSTON, March 10 (AP)—A portrait of President Eisenhower, hung in the exclusive Houston Club, was found slashed last night. A note tacked to the frame said: "We don't like Ike in Texas."

The oil painting by Boris B. Gordon was about a year old. It had been in the club 10 days and was valued at $1,000. Club manager Henry O. Barbour said the painting was to be sent to the Texas Capitol in Austin. Police had no suspects.[14]

---

[13] *New York World-Telegram and The Sun,* July 31, 1957.

[14] *Ibid.,* March 10, 1958.

Boy, 11, Cripples 5 School Buses

DAYTON, Ohio, March 12 (AP)—A fifth-grade boy has admitted that he cut the hydraulic brake lines on five Centerville school buses over the weekend because he was "angry" with a bus driver.

Police said the 11-year-old boy admitted cutting the lines with a pair of snippers because the driver had disciplined him last Wednesday. The vandalism, which knocked out half the fleet of school buses, was discovered Monday during a routine check of the lights and brakes.[15]

Boy, Robbery Foiled, Torments Blind Man

TOCQUIN, Mich., Oct. 20 (UPI)—State police today were looking for a revenge-minded reform school graduate suspected of making life miserable for an elderly blind man and his wife.

The hunted youth "should be tied to a tree and whipped," one trooper said.

About 21 months ago, Thomas D——, 73, and his wife foiled an attempted robbery by two 14-year-old boys of the country store they operate here.

Although blind, Mr. D—— managed to disarm one of the youths who was wielding a shotgun. Mrs. D—— beat the second youth with a broom until he dropped a hunting knife he was brandishing.

The boys fled, but the D—— knew they were from nearby Hartford. State police arrested the youths and they were sent to the Boys Vocational School at Lansing, boasting they would take revenge on the D——.

Both boys were released later. Troopers said one of them has a job and is "going straight."

But the other boy, police said, has been responsible for a series of recent attacks on the D—— property. On seven occasions windows in the D—— store have been broken. Lights have been broken and the store's gasoline pump has been damaged.[16]

---

[15] *Ibid.*, March 12, 1958.

[16] *Ibid.*, October 20, 1959.

The following document reported some years ago in an article about "the urge to destroy" also illustrates vandalism committed for the purpose of "revenge."

> There was a man on our street at home who always sat on his front porch and cursed and swore at everyone who went by. We could never play on the street that he didn't come out and yell at us. On Halloween the kids always used to get back at him. We would write all over his sidewalk and dump his garbage can.
>
> I can honestly say I enjoyed it because he gave everyone so much trouble it was a pleasure to get back at him.[17]

Quite often Vindictive Vandalism occurs as an expression of intergroup tensions which crystallize "when certain minority groups attempt to move into areas populated by a dominant group."[18] The next two documents illustrate willful property destruction in this kind of situation.

> In June of 1931, the owner of a bungalow house on the corner of ——— and ——— Streets moved out of the city leaving the disposal of his property to a real estate agent, Mr. Smith. The neighborhood is a "bungalow district." Most of the houses are reported to be occupied by the owners, who have invested their savings by building their own homes. There are isolated Negro families living within a few blocks of this particular house, but not within the immediate neighborhood. For some years the residents of this district have supported a community improvement association, one purpose of which has been a mutual agreement not to rent or sell property to persons other than members of the Caucasian race. This agreement has been effected by contracts signed by property owners.
>
> A Negro named Mr. Jones, a civil service employee and a World War veteran, was taken by Mr. Smith to look at the property. . . . Shortly afterwards, Mr. Jones signed a contract and made a down payment. . . . The neighbors observed the

[17] W. H. Clark: Sex differences and motivation in the urge to destroy. *The Journal of Social Psychology,* 36 (November, 1952), pp. 167-177.

[18] M. B. Clinard: *Sociology of Deviant Behavior.* New York, Rinehart and Company, 1957, p. 112.

visit of Mr. Jones to the house and began to work out some method of inducing him not to occupy the house. After he had moved his family and possessions into the house, about June 25, the neighbors made various attempts to buy the property from him. To these offers Jones replied he did not buy the property to sell and that he intended to occupy it.

The next development was a series of demonstrations by the neighbors to show their displeasure, in the hope of inducing the family to move. Garbage and refuse of more unpleasant form were hurled on the lawn. Black paint was thrown on the house and garage. Signs were stuck on the premises reading, "We don't want niggers here"; "No niggers allowed in the neighborhood—this means you"; and the like. Mr. Jones took his case to a white attorney, who wrote letters to some of the neighbors, warning them against continuing these disturbances and advising them that if they continued, "Steps would be taken which might prove expensive for them."

Small groups of neighbors began to go by in the evening, shouting jibes and taunts. July 8, about 9:30 P. M., Mr. Jones received an anonymous telephone call, advising him that a mob of five hundred persons would storm their house that night, and warning them to get out. The matter was reported to the neighborhood police station and protection asked for. Frightened by these threats, friends of the family were called in and vigil maintained during the night.

The demonstrations continued, and by Saturday night of that week (July 11) the small groups of protesting neighbors had increased to a crowd of about one hundred fifty.

In the meantime, the colored American Legion Post, of which Mr. Jones is a member, took up the case and stated the annoyances to the city officials and asked for police protection. A conference of white and colored people was called. Each side stated its case. The whites were positive they wanted him out; the Negroes were positive he should not get out but have police protection. The meeting got nowhere.

After this unsuccessful conference, several hundred residents of the neighborhood gathered for a noisy demonstration, irritated because they had no legal recourse and resentful of the attitude shown by the Negroes at the meeting (Tuesday evening). . . .

A mass meeting was called at the neighborhood school building and conciliation was urged (by the civic leaders). . . . During the evening the crowd around the house had been increasing, augmented by curious spectators from all parts of the city, who were attracted by the newspaper reports and eager to see the show. The crowd grew so large and restless that a cordon of police was formed around the place. There was talk of burning the house; of killing and hanging the Negro.

The papers the next day again carried front page stories and that night a crowd of four thousand persons gathered. This was the third large demonstration. (Subsequently the National Association for the Advancement of Colored People entered the case, defended Mr. Jones' property rights, and the neighbors finally settled down to an acceptance of Jones as a neighbor; at least no further demonstrations occurred.)[19]

NEGROES' HOME STONED

Whites Protest in 2 Incidents Near Wilmington, Del.

WILMINGTON, Del., Feb. 24 (AP)—A Negro family moved into the all-white suburb of Collins Park today, touching off two outbreaks. In one the Negroes' home was stoned.

The Negroes, Mr. and Mrs. George R—— and their 14-year-old daughter, moved into their new home at 9:30 A. M. By noon a crowd had surrounded the house.

Mrs. R—— called the State Police, who dispersed the crowd.

After nightfall a crowd reassembled and grew to 300. Stones were thrown and several windows broken.

The State Police with dogs broke up the milling crowd.

Six juveniles and Ronald B——, 20 years old, were arrested.[20]

Sometimes during the course of dominant-minority group disputes the property of minority group leaders is damaged or destroyed. Vindictive Vandalism of this type is illustrated in the next report.

---

[19] From M. Boie: A study of conflict and accommodation in Negro-white relations in the Twin Cities based on documentary sources. Unpublished Master's thesis, University of Minnesota, Minneapolis, 1932. Cited as a description of "social conflict arising from the invasion by Negroes of white territory in Minneapolis" by N. P. Gist and L. A. Halbert: *Urban Society*, fourth edition. New York, Thomas Y. Crowell Company, 1956, pp. 212-214.

[20] *The New York Times*, February 25, 1959.

FOE OF INTEGRATION GETS 6-MONTH TERM

GREENSBORO, N. C., Oct. 8—A 28-year-old carpenter who boasts membership in the Ku Klux Klan was sentenced to a six-month road term today for damaging a Negro lawyer's property.

Clyde A. W—— appealed to Guilford Superior Court after the sentence by Judge William M. P—— of Municipal-County Court.

Judge P—— told W—— and a co-defendant, Roscoe W——, Jr., 17, that they had the right to think and say what they pleased, "but you do not have the right to do as you please."

W—— and W—— had been charged with heaving bottles through windows of the office of Kenneth L——, active in the National Association for the Advancement of Colored People here, and the windows of a barber shop operated by another Negro, Elijah J. H——. . . .[21]

As the following document suggests, in some situations minority people themselves may threaten and damage the property of dominant group members who discriminate against them.

Dominick M—— had been a barber for fourteen years and had a solid trade and a five-chair shop located on Gun Hill Road in the Bronx. In 1952 a low-rent, public housing project was built close by the shop. With the building of this project, Negroes first began to live in the neighborhood which had previously contained only Italian, Irish, and Jewish people.

One day in 1954 a Negro woman came into the shop with her young son. She asked that he be given a haircut. Knowing that a barber he knew had been brought to court by an interracial association when he had refused to cut a Negro's hair, Dominick did not refuse, but gave the boy a haircut.

Thereupon Dominick received a barrage of complaints from his customers. He lost some of his newer customers. However, he had no more Negro trade until early in 1955 when a Negro boy about sixteen years old came in and asked for a haircut. The shop was crowded with whites at the time, but the boy waited. When his turn came, Dominick accepted him smilingly, but then just before starting to cut his hair he said to him in a

[21] *Ibid.*, October 9, 1958.

grave tone, "Your hair is too dirty and greasy. I can't cut it." The boy walked out without a word. The customers in the shop congratulated Dominick on the way he had handled the situation. All was well for about two hours when the same Negro boy walked in again. This time his hair was "bone dry" as though he had washed it while he had been away from the shop. This time Dominick told him that he could not cut his hair because he did not know how to cut his type of hair. It was too "kinky." The boy gave a meaningful glance at Dominick's hair, which was also curly and "kinky," and walked out. He returned in about a minute accompanied by a Jewish lawyer, a Chinese, and a Negro man, who identified themselves as members of the same interracial association that had previously brought Dominick's barber friend into court.

Dominick picked up a razor and threatened to throw them all out, but after they said to him, "You have a nice place here, barber, we would hate to see it ruined," Dominick cut the boy's hair. But he literally "butchered" it. The delegation left without a word.

About a month later, Dominick's barber shop was broken into. Mirrors were broken. The leather seat on one of the barber chairs was slashed. And other things were damaged. Little of value was stolen.

Meanwhile, Dominick had lost some of his white trade. But this was to be expected.

Almost a year later, another Negro woman brought her young child into the shop for a haircut. This time Dominick did not refuse, but "butchered" the boy's hair by cutting "steps" into it and what not. The next morning Dominick received a threatening note which he found slipped under the door of his shop. The note said in part, "You'd better be careful or there will be some s——t spilt." That night the shop was "hit" for the second time and considerable damage was done. All the razors were stolen and every bottle of soap and hair tonic was either broken or emptied into the sink and toilet.

Since the second vandalism, Dominick has continued to "butcher" the hair of Negroes who sometimes come to him for haircuts, even of one who keeps coming in as a regular customer. But his shop has not been damaged again.[22]

[22] From a written statement given to the author by a young man who had close personal knowledge of the incidents described.

On other occasions, as the following incident shows, property damage arising from dominant-minority group tensions is not directed against the personal property of either minority or dominant group members, but against "symbolic" property, such as synagogues and cemeteries.

> Temple Ohabed Zedek, 954 ——— Avenue, is part of a two-family house. The rabbi and his family lived upstairs. Windows were broken in the synagogue on the nights of March 9, 10, 11 and 16, 1943. Vandalism stopped when a policeman was stationed outside. Five members of a gang were arrested. . . .
>
> (One of them) K. D., eighteen, testified that he had broken windows "to try to get the Jews off the block." In 1941 he had broken into a store window owned by Jews and stolen money, cigarettes and shoes. Caught and held delinquent, he blames Jews because the store was "Jewish." He said his gang believed Jews were no good in the war, they were "yellow." K. D. had transferred to high school from a parochial school. He left school at sixteen. . . .[23]

Vindictive Vandalism of this type is well illustrated by the numerous anti-Semitic acts in various countries which were conspicuously reported in the press during the winter of 1959-1960. Starting in West Germany with the defacing of a Cologne synagogue on Christmas Eve, this wave of anti-Semitic vandalism rapidly spread with a kind of "emotional contagion" to much of Europe, the British Isles, North and South America, Australia, and other parts of the world.

At its height this outbreak involved more than the desecration of synagogues and Jewish cemeteries. Nazi swastikas and anti-Semitic slogans appeared on a variety of other kinds of property. A few Christian churches were also defaced. And in some communities Jews were jeered at, taunted, and threatened. But the principal theme was the desecration of property sacred to Jews.

---

[23] From a description of vandalism in New York City in S. Tenenbaum: *Why Men Hate.* New York, The Beechhurst Press, 1947, p. 104. (Reprinted by permission)

A few of the scores of incidents which happened in New York City and in other parts of the United States are described in the following news stories.

SWASTIKA PAINTED ON TEMPLE EMANU-EL

24-Hour Guard Posted by Police;
3 Similar Incidents in Queens

Temple Emanu-El, Fifth Ave. and 65th St., the largest Jewish house of worship in the United States, was under round-the-clock police guard yesterday after a four-foot-high black swastika was found painted on the wall of the 65th St. side.

A few hours after police had scrubbed the temple's wall clean of the Nazi symbol, similar desecrations were discovered in Queens on a synagogue, a Jewish center, and the former quarters of a Jewish veterans' organization. . . .[24]

DESECRATION IN PHILADELPHIA

PHILADELPHIA, Jan. 6—Three swastikas were smeared in gray paint on the walls of Congregation Rodeph Shalom here last night. It was the first incident in this city in the current wave of anti-Semitic acts.[25]

5 YOUTHS SEIZED AS SWASTICADS WHO DEFACED PARK FIELD HOUSE

Five teen-agers were rounded up in Queens yesterday in the painting of swastikas and the scrawl, "Down With Jews," on the field house of Bowne Park, 157th St. and 32d Ave., Flushing, Queens, shortly after midnight. . . .[26]

Some insight into the deeply-rooted Jewish-Christian tension that may periodically find expression in anti-Semitic vandalism is provided by the following document.

The Jewish element was located in one block. The Irish element was located in another block. . . . I have known a

[24] *New York Herald-Tribune,* January 4, 1960.
[25] *The New York Times,* January 7, 1960.
[26] *New York Daily News,* January 11, 1960.

couple of occasions where we actually fought each other (with snow balls). And I can recall one instance where it actually was a gang type thing. . . .

I don't think that we actually considered ourselves as "hostile" to one another, although in private conversations and so forth we often made derogatory remarks about the Jews. . . . I do know of an instance where a remark was made to an Irish kid. We had jackets with "SH" (standing for Sacred Heart School which informant attended) on them. One Jewish kid said to this fellow, "Why don't you complete the word? Add '—I—T'." The Irish kid pulverized him. . . .

One evening, a few of the boys in my school actually performed acts of vandalism against the Jewish synagogue in the neighborhood. . . . They threw tomatoes and old oranges—some fruit which they got from garbage cans—at the synagogue. . . . Similar acts had occurred in the past. . . .

What did you people think about the incident? We probably thought it was funny. . . . If it (had happened) to the Catholic church, much more aggressive behavior would have occurred between the Jew and the Catholic. I am positive that there definitely would have been a number of more fights and a great deal more damage done to the synagogue. . . . Although with the Jew, I would not expect them to react in the same way in an aggressive fashion.

Why? Because in all our dealings they seemed to be rather timid. . . . I think that's one reason why I have always considered the Jew to be somewhat of a coward. Although in the army, I had some Jewish friends of mine who by no means were cowards.[27]

Aside from interracial and interreligious tensions, Vindictive Vandalism sometimes arises out of the tensions and antagonisms of international politics. "Revengeful" vandalism of this type is illustrated in the following report.

---

[27] From an interview by the author with a college student who grew up in the Bronx, New York City.

ATTACK RED OFFICE HERE

3 Aliens Hurl Bottles at Panes
in Soviet U. N. Headquarters

Three persons who said they were of Hungarian extraction were arrested last night, accused of throwing soda bottles at the headquarters of the Soviet delegation to the United Nations, 680 Park Avenue.

The two women and a man, all aliens, told the police they had become aroused after hearing a radio news broadcast about the Hungarian situations. Armed with a dozen bottles of soda each, they went to the building at the corner of East Sixty-eighth Street and began throwing the missiles at windows, the police said. One ground-floor window was broken before the three were seized by a policeman on duty near by. . . .[28]

Sometimes, as the following incident shows, "spiteful" damage occurs in industrial plants as the result of a worker's grudge against management.

L. I. WORKER HELD IN ATOMIC DAMAGE

U. S. Says He Struck Reactor Parts
With File to Spite Hicksville Employer

An amateur weight lifter who works in a Long Island plant that makes uranium-filled cylinders for the Government atomic energy program was accused yesterday of damaging them to spite his employer.

The husky defendant, Santo S—— of 125 ——— Road, New Hyde Park, L. I., was arraigned before United States Commissioner Martin C. Epstein in Brooklyn Federal Court on a charge of destroying Government property.

He could have been charged with sabotage, a much more serious offense, according to Kenneth C. Sternberg, chief of the criminal division of the United States Attorney's office. But Mr. Sternberg said the Government was satisfied that the 45-year-old defendant had not considered the possible far-reaching effects of his destructive work. . . .

The defendant's growing anger, Mr. Sternberg said, began

[28] *The New York Times,* October 29, 1956.

with an accident when he was a machine operator. The end of his left little finger had to be amputated. This spoiled his hobby of lifting weights.

His employer, the ——— Corporation in Hicksville, put him on light duty. Then Mr. S—— was made the subject of an extensive poster campaign in the factory to promote safety on the job, Mr. Sternberg said. As Mr. S—— recalled to Mr. Sternberg, his picture was on the poster over a message to this effect: "Make sure it doesn't happen to you." . . .

Several days after the poster appeared, Mr. S—— was put to work with a sprayer, a one-handed job, Mr. Sternberg quoted the defendant. He decided to get even for what he considered indignities, the lawyer said.

When no one was looking, Mr. Sternberg said, the defendant would strike a uranium slug with a metal file. The bad slugs were soon detected and Mr. S—— was caught with the help of a movie camera. . . .[29]

More frequently, however, willful damage to industrial and business property occurs during the course of the more traditional conflict between workers and management during union attempts to organize workers or negotiate new contracts. The next documents illustrate vandalism as it commonly occurs in such situations.

Bakery in Dispute Is Damaged by Acid

The Queens District Attorney began investigation yesterday of vandalism directed at a Queens bakery having labor trouble.

The latest incident occurred Sunday evening when hydrofluoric acid was splashed on six windows and a glass door of the B—— Pastry Shop, ——— Street, Flushing. The acid, which is used in etching glass, caused $1,500 to $2,000 damage, according to the owner, Joseph C. B——.

Mr. B—— owns four pastry shops in Queens and Manhattan. He said that all had been picketed since last November by two

---

[29] *Ibid.*, November 30, 1957.

For a more detailed consideration of industrial vandalism of this type undertaken in response to personal resentment, *see* Vandalism: Rehearsal for sabotage? *Business Week,* July 5, 1952, pp. 72-74.

Case material already presented about Sidney,[49] one of two participants in another of the five incidents, further illuminates the role that conflict between children and school personnel may play in the destruction of school property. In this affair, in which a school library was the principal target, Sidney, one of two Jewish boys involved, "wanted revenge" on the school librarian because he felt "that she was 'badgering' him about overdue books." The other boy participated because he thought that it was his chance to "get even" with the librarian whom he felt "didn't like Jewish kids."

The next document describes anti-Semitic vandalism as experienced by a member of a victim's family. The document tells of an episode—another of the five incidents of Vindictive Vandalism committed by the Children's Court vandals surveyed in this study—in which Puerto Rican boys repeatedly smashed the windows in a rabbi's home.[50]

> Rabbi Epstein and his family have lived in their neighborhood for over twenty years and in their present ground-floor apartment for the past eighteen years. At one time the neighborhood was largely composed of Jewish and Irish families. Recently, however, many of these families have moved elsewhere and have been replaced by Negroes and especially Puerto Ricans. At present most of the families living in the Epstein apartment building are Puerto Rican. Other nearby buildings are crowded with Puerto Rican and Negro people.
>
> One of Rabbi Epstein's sons, a medical student at Yeshiva University, clearly recalled the time the windows were broken in his family's apartment. He said the windows had been "systematically broken" over a period of several weeks by Puerto Rican boys living in the neighborhood, and that at one time or another the windows and property of other Jewish people living in the neighborhood had also been damaged. He believed that such destruction was an expression of the "tension" that existed in the neighborhood and he wondered whether the incidents in

---

49 See Case Three, Chapter III, pp. 42-46.

50 For case material about one of the boys involved in this vandalism, see Case One, Chapter III, pp. 32-37.

which his family's windows had been broken had been instigated by adult Puerto Ricans who were trying to get the rabbi to move out so that they might have the family apartment. The rabbi's son said the neighborhood had changed greatly in recent years. For example, he said that when he was a boy, he customarily wore his *yamulka* (skull cap) out on the street However, nowadays he cautioned his younger brother against doing this since it was likely to provoke "incidents." He also commented that when he was out on the street he frequently heard, as he passed them by, even young Puerto Rican children say, as they looked up at him, "Oh! You killed our God!"[51]

The last four of the twelve incidents could be classified as Wanton Vandalism: in one public school property was destroyed; another involved the breaking of windows and bottles in the rear of an apartment house; the third involved damage to automobiles; while the fourth involved damage to shop equipment and the destruction of office supplies.

It appeared that one of the four incidents was simply "playful" destruction, while another was a prime example of property destruction by youths "at war" with the community. The two remaining incidents apparently fell somewhere between the two extremes.

Case material already presented about Frankie,[52] one of the boys who participated in the incident in which shop equipment was damaged and office supplies destroyed, outlines the kind of situation in which the frolicsome activity of boys exploring new environments may lead to the "playful" destruction of property. The two young brothers entered a shop in their slum neighborhood one afternoon "to see what it was like"; tried to start some of the machines, damaging them in the process; "messed up" the office looking for something to steal; and playfully scattered a box of pencils around the room amid cries of "Merry Christmas." Prior to this affair, as the case material indicates, the brothers had engaged in other vandalism including that which occurred during their explorations of a local "pickle factory"

---

51 From observations and an interview by the author.

52 See Case Five, Chapter III, pp. 53-58.

where together with their sister and cousin, they had damaged property during the excitement of a "pickle fight."

The next document, which relates to the incident in which automobiles were damaged, represents Wanton Vandalism of an opposite kind. The report describes property destruction by a gang of youths on the rampage in the community.

OFFICER'S SHOT BREAKS UP TEENAGE HOODLUM ATTACK

A group of teenage hoodlums who had been drinking and amusing themselves by jumping on the hoods of parked cars, attacked a police lieutenant in the Bronx early yesterday when he broke up their pastime.

Lt. James O—— seized the gang leader when the half dozen youths jumped him. He fired a warning shot in the air to frighten off his attackers and police, attracted by the shot, captured a second gang member. Both boys are 15 and will be brought to Children's Court today on delinquency charges.

The officer was returning in civilian clothes to his home at 154 ——— Avenue, Bronxchester (a middle-class housing development), after finishing his 4 PM-to-midnight duty at the Wakefield Station when he saw the gang kicking in the sides of cars and jumping up and down on hoods at ——— Road and ——— Drive.

As he approached, Lt. O—— heard one youth say, "Let's go to Bronxchester and kick the ——— out of cops." He recognized the gang as neighborhood hoodlums who have been carrying on guerrilla warfare against the special officers at the housing project.

"Then they saw me and said, 'This guy's following us. Let's get him,'" Lt. O—— said. "I identified myself and grabbed one of them. They jumped me and tried to pull him loose. I fired a warning shot and they ran. I'd hate to have been an unarmed civilian then."

Within five minutes, police responded to the shot and arrested a second gang member. The one Lt. O—— had held on to during the melee kicked the officer in the shins. Lt. O—— reported the gang "all had some drink in them." The two under arrest were not identified by police because of their age.[53]

---

[53] *New York Herald-Tribune*, June 13, 1955.

Case material already presented about Hugh,[54] one of the youths arrested in this affair, further illuminates the situation in which this incident occurred. As the material indicates, several of the youths involved went out looking for somebody to "beat up" and "rob" in a middle-class housing development after they had run out of money one night while drinking at a local bar. They were also going to "beat up" a member of the housing development police force with which they had been in prolonged conflict. During their foray through the development, as the case material indicates, they "jumped on a few cars and broke a few windows." The youths then attacked the New York City police lieutenant who accosted them and arrested their leader.

The following document presents a participant's version of another of the four incidents of Wanton Vandalism committed by Children's Court vandals surveyed in this study. The document, which refers to an episode in which public school property was destroyed, describes one of the two incidents of Wanton Vandalism that appeared to be part play and part "malicious" destruction.

> I was in the school yard and Joey[55] went in and opened the door. So a few of my friends went in and I went in with them. Somebody said, "Let's break the winders." He had a stickball bat. Later we went over to the papers—stacks of newspapers up against the wall—and we threw them around the place. So after I went out of the school and went in the school garden where my cousin (one of the other boys involved) was. I think it was about at least ten minutes went by and I heard things being smashed. You know, like when a winder breaks. A few of my friends went out into the garden and got rocks and threw them at the light globes. So I went back in and I saw that there were winders, light globes, and colored glass winders in the auditorium broken. At night of the same day—this happened in the daytime—a fire extinguisher got squirted all over the place.

---

[54] See Case Six, Chapter III, pp. 59-65.

[55] For case material about Joey, see Case Two, Chapter III, pp. 38-42.

Were you with them when this happened? No. I was upstairs. My father wouldn't let me come out at night.

A few days later I was in school and a teacher and another guy came and they sent for me out of the classroom. I went up to the office and they started talkin' to me. And they asked me, "Who damaged the things in the school?" I didn't mention nobody's name, but yet they got us one at a time. They sent for Vinnie (another boy involved in the incident) and they started asking him questions. I think it must have been about three weeks later the same boy came into the classroom and said for me to get my coat and my books and go down to the office. So I went down to the office and I see a flatfoot—a cop. There was two of them. Two cops. They started askin' my friends and me questions. So we got in the car and went down to Tuccillo's school (another boy involved in the incident). The cop went inside to get him and he wasn't there. He played hookey that day. The cop came back and said to his friend that Tuccillo wasn't there. So they took us down to the 156th Precinct. Oh yeah! So then either our mothers or fathers had to come and get us out. They told us to report to court, I think two days later. The judge gave us all probation, except for one guy. He got nuthin'. Two got away.

What happened to Joey? Oh yeah! He didn't get nothin' neither. I just remembered that.

Why did you go into the school in the first place? To have fun. They thought it was a big joke breakin' things. Somebody said, "Let's break the winders."[56]

---

[56] From an interview by the author.

Chapter V

THE PREVENTION OF VANDALISM

Because . . . social phenomena are so forbidding, or at least so seem, and because they yield few hard tests of what exists and what does not, they afford to the individual a luxury not given by physical phenomena. Within a considerable range he is permitted to believe what he pleases. He may hold whatever view of this world he finds most agreeable or otherwise to his taste.

JOHN KENNETH GALBRAITH, *The Affluent Society*

IT IS clear from the comparisons between vandals and other delinquents made in Chapter II that in terms of their sex, age, and ethnic characteristics vandals appear to differ from other delinquents. They are far more likely to be males, are younger, and, although as with other delinquents they are mostly white, comparisons with other delinquents indicate that among vandals whites are over-represented, non-whites are under-represented, while Puerto Ricans are but slightly over-represented.

Further comparisons between vandals and other delinquents revealed, however, that both seem to live in the same kinds of urban areas or neighborhoods: the percentage distribution of both uniformly increased as the socio-economic level of their areas of residence decreased; almost half of both groups lived in the poorest and most deteriorated areas.

Nevertheless, in addition to differences in their sex, age, and ethnic characteristics, vandals apparently differ from other delinquents in several other respects. Their families seem to be characterized by more parent-child conflict and hostility than the families of other delinquents. The families of vandals also appear to be much less mobile. And, finally, vandalism itself, even more than other male delinquency, seems to be almost exclusively a group offense.

Another conclusion to be drawn from this research is that both vandals and vandalism may be classified according to subtypes. Thus in Chapter III vandals were classified as *Disturbed, Essentially Law-Abiding,* and *Subcultural,* while in Chapter IV vandalism itself was divided into *Predatory, Vindictive,* and *Wanton* types of property destruction.

The basic characteristics of Disturbed Vandals are their gross personality disturbance and their repeated delinquency, while Essentially Law-Abiding Vandals are distinguished by their absence of serious mental disturbance and by the fact that their lapse into vandalism is quite incidental to their otherwise nondelinquent careers. On the other hand, Subcultural Vandals, although not characterized by gross mental pathology, are "career delinquents" with histories of frequent participation in various kinds of group delinquency.

Predatory Vandalism seems essentially to be undertaken for the purpose of acquiring "scarce goods," as in some forms of "junking" or in smashing store windows in order to steal merchandise on display. Vindictive Vandalism appears primarily to be committed for revengeful or spiteful purposes against particular individuals or groups, as in settling a grudge or in damaging the property of racial or religious minority groups. Wanton Vandalism is somewhat more complex. At one extreme, Wanton Vandalism seems to occur simply as part of the play activity of young children. At the other, it seems to be spontaneous and wild destruction by groups of marauding youths who are in open conflict with the community.

Although the general public frequently condemns vandalism as the "senseless" destruction of property, one of the most important conclusions to be derived from the present study is that vandalism of the types described in Chapter IV is both meaningful to the participants and understandable in terms of the situations in which it occurs.

Donald R. Taft has suggested that most crime is an expression of a conflict relationship and that standing behind the immediate conflict between the criminal and his victim lies conflict between law-breakers on the one hand, and the agencies which enforce or administer the criminal law, on the other.[1]

So, too, with vandalism: Vindictive Vandalism represents a direct and open expression of conflict between vandals and particular persons and groups, as well as conflict between vandals and community agencies which attempt to prevent violations of the normative standards regarding property set forth in the criminal law and endorsed by the larger community. In this sense Predatory Vandalism also represents conflict—conflict between vandals and their values regarding the property rights of others, and the police and other community agencies attempting to enforce the rules against the violation of such rights. Lastly, Wanton Vandalism, particularly the destruction wrought by marauding adolescent groups, also becomes meaningful when seen as conflict—again conflict between such groups and their values, on the one hand, and the community and its values, on the other.

Explicit in this research has been the theoretical position that to understand the "whys" of vandalism we must look to the characteristics of the juveniles who commit such delinquency, to their home life, to their peer group relationships, to both the "objective" and "subjective" aspects of the situations in which vandalism occurs, and to the local milieu which supplies the situations within which vandals react. However, to achieve a more complete understanding of vandalism, as well as of the conflict that it represents, it is now necessary to go beyond the study of children, their families, peer groups, and neighborhood and to examine the root characteristics of American society which appear to foster vandalism and other types of crime and delinquency. In brief we must explore "the impelling forces to delinquency (which) inhere deeply in the culture of the American people."[2]

The importance of such exploration must not be overlooked. To do so is simply to avoid a basic dimension in the study of delinquency. Noting the emphasis placed on the milieu and the

---

[1] D. R. Taft: *Criminology,* third edition. New York, The Macmillan Company, 1956, pp. 26-27.

[2] M. L. Barron: *The Juvenile in Delinquent Society.* New York, Alfred A. Knopf, 1954, p. 201.

neglect given the larger social structure in psychological and social psychological studies of human behavior, Robert K. Merton has suggested that in the study of juvenile delinquency:

> Observation of the milieu is theoretically essential, but it is not sufficient. It is essential because the pressures of the larger social structure are mediated through the intervening structure. But useful as it is, the tendency to focus on the immediate milieu (the patterns of interpersonal relations in which individuals are directly involved) has led to relative neglect of the larger social structure.[3]

Clinard has drawn attention to the role played by the larger society in the development of delinquency.[4] He has noted that, while delinquency is relatively rare in folk societies characterized by a consistent value structure, the inconsistent value patterns typical of the adult world in societies such as our own constitute one of the chief moral hazards to juveniles. "It is," according to Clinard, "obviously impossible to rear law-abiding children in a world where adult models disobey the law."

The relationship between crime and delinquency and the American way of life is even more poignantly suggested in the writings of other sociologists. Thus, in writing of crime in general, Taft has called attention to the "criminogenic" features of American culture.[5] He has stated that, among its other traits, American culture is both dynamic and complex. It is also materialistic and increasingly impersonal. Because of its heterogeneity, it fosters restricted group loyalties. Furthermore it still extols the frontier values of extreme individualism, assertiveness, and violence.

Thus life in the United States stands, for example, in sharp

---

[3] R. K. Merton: The social-cultural environment and *anomie,* in H. L. Witmer and R. Kotinsky (eds.): *New Perspectives for Research on Juvenile Delinquency.* Children's Bureau, United States Department of Health, Education, and Welfare, Publication 356. Washington, Government Printing Office, 1956, pp. 24-50.

[4] M. B. Clinard: Secondary community influences and juvenile delinquency. *The Annals of The American Academy of Political and Social Science,* 261 (January, 1949), pp. 42-53.

[5] Taft, *op. cit.,* pp. 38-43.

contrast with the life of the European peasant who lived in an entirely different type of social and cultural situation, but one which, whether we care to admit it or not, was relatively crimeless.[6] For such a man "there were no loose, disordered ends; everything was knotted into a firm relationship with every other thing"; he was firmly attached to his fellow villagers by relationships, ties, family, kinship, and many rights and obligations—all of which had meaning in terms of life as a whole.[7] In essence, although perhaps "uncivilized" to contemporary Americans comfortable in their materialism, the unchanging village culture of peasant Europe contained "built-in" inhibitors to crime and delinquency, whereas American society, a mélange of changing people, customs, and morals, offers rich opportunity for the occurrence of law violation as a manifestation of personal and social disorganization.

The first case study presented in this research aptly illustrates this proposition.[8] It describes the delinquency, including the vandalism, of a young Puerto Rican migrant who was living a disordered and rootless existence in a New York slum, isolated from family, school, church, and even friends. The youngster was finally committed to a state hospital as a violently paranoid schizophrenic. His vandalism, an expression of his anti-Semitism, involved breaking the windows in the home of a neighborhood rabbi. This destruction occurred in a rapidly changing part of the Bronx torn by marked Jewish-Christian tension arising from the invasion by Puerto Ricans and Negroes of a former Jewish-Irish neighborhood. Had this child remained in his home town of Ponce in Puerto Rico, he might or might not have become violently psychotic and he might or might not have become delinquent. But in any case, it is almost certain that in Ponce—where the few Jews are largely of the professional and business class and where there is only one rabbi[9]—this boy would not have be-

---

[6] *Ibid.*, pp. 21-22.

[7] O. Handlin: *The Uprooted.* New York, Grosset and Dunlap Publishers, pp. 8-9.

[8] See Case One, Chapter III, pp. 32-37.

[9] This description of the Jewish population in Ponce was given to the author by a sociologist who is long familiar with the city and acquainted with the rabbi who resides there.

come involved in the invasion of a former Jewish-Irish neighborhood and that his aggression would not have found a handy target in the home of a nearby rabbi. For this he had to migrate to Nueva York.

Briefly the point is this: *juvenile delinquency, including juvenile vandalism, cannot be understood unless it is related to the total social matrix within which it occurs.*[10] This is scarcely the whole story, but it is the place at which a really meaningful analysis must begin or end, depending upon whether the social system or the individual is used as the point of departure.

Further reference to the criminogenic features of the American social system has been made by Merton in his discussion of "Social Structure and Anomie."[11] In writing particularly of crimes for economic gain, he has suggested that American culture approximates the type in which great emphasis is placed on the achievement of "success" without equivalent emphasis being placed on institutional means: what counts is "winning the game" instead of "winning under the rules of the game." And the game, of course, is the accumulation of money. This deification of money as a symbol of success makes strong demands upon individuals located at all levels of our economic system, but the demands are especially frustrating to those at the lower level. On the one hand, unlike lower-class people in a more rigid class system, they are exhorted to better themselves by competing for and winning the grandest prize of all: money! On the other, their class position largely denies them effective opportunities for attaining this goal. "In this setting," according to Merton, "a cardinal American virtue, 'ambition,' promotes a cardinal American vice, 'deviant behavior.' "[12]

[10] For an excellent discussion of this point as it applies to various American and non-American territories, see *Juvenile Delinquency in Non-Self-Governing Territories.* Report to the Secretariat. New York, United Nations General Assembly, A/AC .35/L.270, 17 March, 1958, especially pp. 8-10.

This report stated that differences in social organization and cultural pattern accounted for the fact that while in American Samoa and many tribal areas of Africa and Southeast Asia juvenile delinquency is virtually non-existent, it has long been a problem of considerable concern in places like Hawaii, Hong Kong, and Singapore.

[11] R. K. Merton: *Social Theory and Social Structure.* Glencoe, Illinois, The Free Press, 1949, chap. IV.

[12] *Ibid.*, p. 137.

Although perhaps more easily understood when applied to our labor racketeers, professional bootleggers, and big-time bookies, this analysis seems to apply with equal validity to our lesser criminals and delinquents whose offenses also involve material gain. Thus it is suggestive of how various types of delinquency, including certain kinds of Predatory Vandalism, reflect the basic characteristics of our social system.

In attempting to explain the origins of what he calls the "non-utilitarian, malicious, negativistic, versatile, hedonistic, and autonomous" behavior of working-class gang boys, Cohen has proposed that such behavior is also to be accounted for in terms of the stresses and tensions of American society.[13] He has hypothesized that the behavior of such groups is a consequence of the hostility working-class boys feel for middle-class values, such as ambition, courtesy, opposition to physical violence, and respect for property. According to this theory, working-class boys resent such dominant values because they are not part of their social world, and because, lacking these virtues, such boys are assigned low status by "the people who count" such as school teachers, social workers, and other middle-class representatives. Thus working-class delinquent gangs, Cohen has argued, are a natural consequence of boys of this class coming together because of shared hostilities to create a situation in which they can achieve status by excelling at the very behaviors condemned by middle-class society, while at the same time striking back at the community which has so deeply offended them. "What the (working-class gang) delinquent does," according to Cohen, "is not merely right by his standards; it is right because it is wrong by conventional standards."[14]

This analysis, too, is strongly indicative of how the taproots of vandalism, particularly the Wanton Vandalism committed by

---

[13] A. K. Cohen: *Delinquent Boys: The Culture of the Gang.* Glencoe, Illinois, The Free Press, 1955.

The summary of Cohen's theory presented here was adapted, in part, from M. B. Clinard: *Sociology of Deviant Behavior.* New York, Rinehart and Company, 1957, p. 183.

[14] Quoted by M. E. Blake: *Youth Groups in Conflict.* Children's Bureau, United States Department of Health, Education, and Welfare, Publication 365. Washington, Government Printing Office, 1958, p. 7.

working-class gangs in open conflict with the community, may lie deep in the heart of our social system. Although these statements offer little insight into wanton destruction committed by middle-class boys,[15] they do provide a provocative theory to explain the wanton and malicious destruction so frequently wrought by working-class gangs in our communities.

Quite contrary to Cohen, Bloch and Niederhoffer view the gang not as a phenomenon rooted in interclass tension and conflict, but as one that arises to meet the sociological and psychological stresses of adolescence.[16] They have proposed that under the right conditions adolescent gangs develop in both primitive and modern societies. Thus:

> When a society does not make adequate preparation, formal or otherwise, for the induction of its adolescents to adult status, equivalent forms of behavior (gangs) arise spontaneously among adolescents themselves, reinforced by their own group structure, which seemingly provides the same psychological content and function as the more formalized rituals (puberty rites) found in other societies.[17]

Bloch and Niederhoffer readily admit, however, that the stresses of adolescence are particularly acute in American society and that class membership can affect gang behavior as when attitudes toward fighting and aggression and lack of regard for property enter into the choice of delinquent acts by lower-class boys.[18]

---

[15] For a brief and tentative explanation of the delinquency, including the vandalism, committed by middle-class boys, see Cohen, *op. cit., pp.* 162-169. Here Cohen, utilizing a formulation by Talcott Parsons, suggests that middle-class male delinquency may stem from a boy's attempt to gain recognition as a male. As Parsons states, child-rearing practices in the American family, which place heavy emphasis on the mother's role in socialization and transmission of traditional canons of good behavior to the child, may cause the middle-class male adolescent to reject "goodness," which he associates with femininity, and to embrace "badness" in his attempt to establish himself as a male. Thus Cohen conceives of middle-class male delinquency as primarily an attempt to cope with a basic anxiety in the area of sex-role identification.

[16] H. A. Bloch and A. Niederhoffer: *The Gang: A Study in Adolescent Behavior.* New York, Philosophical Library, 1958.

[17] *Ibid.,* p. 17.

[18] *Ibid.,* pp. 30 and 182.

To the extent that the theories of Clinard, Taft, and the others have merit in explaining the social and cultural foundations of delinquency in the United States, then any *large-scale* reductions in the amount of vandalism, as well as other types of delinquency, in our society are unlikely unless substantial reforms are effected which at present we may either lack the skill to achieve or, possessing the skill, might well reject. Pushing this to the extreme, how many Americans would want to imitate the life of peasant Europe even if they somehow could reverse the twin processes of industrialization and urbanization? How many would want to forego the benefits of mass production and a wondrously high standard of living even if delinquency is part of the price we must pay for such luxury?

Furthermore, to the degree that vandalism and other kinds of delinquency spring from the basic characteristics of American society, any conclusion that, "The roots of delinquency lie in the home!" must be rejected, as must the numerous other beguiling explanations which clutter the history of criminology. Such a conclusion must be rejected not because it is untrue, but because so much else that is both pertinent and true is omitted and even denied by those who champion this interpretation of delinquency. While it is quite obvious that socialization within the family is of crucial importance in child development, the family, particularly in urban life, is scarcely the only socializing agency. The school and the peer group also play significant parts in socialization. Moreover, and this point seems to have escaped those who explain delinquency principally in terms of family inadequacy and strain, "families, schools, and peer groups do not operate *in vacuo*."[19] In large measure all simply reflect the neighborhoods, and, in turn, the societies in which they are found.

The aim of this, the concluding chapter in the present study, is two-fold: (1) to evaluate some of the many programs and devices that have been offered for the prevention of delinquency

---

[19] J. H. S. Bossard: *The Sociology of Child Development,* revised edition. New York, Harper and Brothers, 1954, p. 550.

in general, as well as some that have been offered for the prevention of vandalism as a type of delinquency; and (2) in view of the characteristics of vandals and vandalism described in earlier parts of this research, to make recommendations regarding programs especially appropriate for preventing vandalism.

EVALUATION OF DELINQUENCY PREVENTION PROGRAMS

Granting the improbability of obtaining large-scale reductions in the amount of vandalism and other types of delinquency without achieving substantial, but unlikely, social reforms, nonetheless a variety of less ambitious schemes have been proposed as means for reducing the incidence of juvenile misconduct.

Two of the most popular, and at the same time most controversial, have been proposals for curfews and proposals for punishing the parents of delinquents. Each has been spiritedly defended, just as each has been vigorously condemned. Usually those who urge a curfew also support the idea of parental punishment, while those who oppose one also oppose the other. In essence, such controversy is just another aspect of the traditional debate between those who favor repression or punishment as a general policy for preventing crime, and those who favor treatment or rehabilitation. Unfortunately no decisive, empirically-derived proof exists regarding the relative efficacy of the two policies. As Sutherland has succinctly pointed out, those who favor punishment "can muster as much evidence for their position as can those who favor treatment policies."[20] So the debate continues.

Two recent publications are useful in appraising the merits of curfews as devices for preventing vandalism and other types of delinquency. The first is a survey by the New York State Youth Commission of curfew ordinances as they exist and are used in New York municipalities.[21] The study found that 44, or 40 per cent, of 110 responding municipalities had local laws or ordi-

[20] E. H. Sutherland: Control of crime, in A. Cohen, *et al.* (eds.): *The Sutherland Papers.* Bloomington, Indiana University Press, 1956, pp. 167-172.

[21] *A Study of Curfew Ordinances in New York State.* Albany, New York State Youth Commission, December, 1957.

nances making it unlawful for a child under a specific age, usually sixteen, to remain on the streets between certain hours at night and in the morning. The most common curfew hour was found to be 10:00 P. M. Most of the laws exempt children accompanied by a parent, guardian, or other person having legal control or custody, or children employed or on an errand. The majority of the ordinances had been passed since 1940, but some had been adopted as early as 1900-1910. Most of the municipalities reported that their ordinances were not generally enforced. Usually the laws provide penalties for children who remain out after curfew and for parents who permit their children to violate the curfew.

In appraising these ordinances the Commission concluded that most of the curfew laws in New York communities are "inadequate, unrealistic and outmoded." The Commission further noted that unless communities want to clear all of their children off the streets at night, they can achieve desired night-time control without curfews by enforcement of already existing general State laws. Included in such general laws are sections of the New York Penal Law which prohibit disorderly conduct and unlawful assemblies, and which forbid parents and guardians to contribute to the delinquency of their children by allowing them to wander about the streets late at night.

An article in the *National Probation and Parole Association Journal* is also useful for appraising curfew ordinances.[22] The article used these words to describe the basic nature of the debate between those who favor and those who oppose curfews:

> One group assumes that a relationship exists between a curfew and the number of delinquent acts committed by children after the curfew hour, the other insists that keeping children off the streets at night is of no value because it fails to change those basic attitudes and values which determine behavior. Neither of these two assumptions can be verified to any degree because of insufficient research on the subject.

---

[22] F. L. Manella: Curfew laws. *NPPA Journal,* 4 (April, 1958), pp. 161-168.

Complementing one of the basic conclusions reached by the New York State Youth Commission study, the article also quoted the Chief of the Technical Aid Branch of the U. S. Children's Bureau to the effect that "if the power is already provided for in other ordinances, the answer is not a curfew but better law enforcement."

Finally, questioning the legality of curfew ordinances, the article cited two recent court decisions in California and Florida which found specific curfew ordinances to be unconstitutional. In California, the Third District Court of Appeals found that the ordinance of the City of Chico "went too far in that it prohibited the 'mere presence of a minor on the street unless accompanied by a parent or guardian.'" This, the court held, was "an arbitrary invasion of inherent personal rights." In Florida, a circuit court made a similar finding when it ruled that a Miami curfew ordinance was "unconstitutional, arbitrary, unreasonable, and discriminatory"; and "the city of Miami was permanently enjoined in the final decree from enforcing the provisions of the curfew ordinance."

In sum, despite the exhortations to adopt curfew laws, their value is at best speculative. In addition, special curfew ordinances may in fact be unnecessary if provision is made in state law for the night-time control of wandering children, unless a community wishes to keep all of its children off its streets at night. In the latter case, judicial decisions have raised serious doubt as to the constitutionality of local ordinances adopted for this purpose.

That juvenile curfews are very likely unconstitutional may be difficult for some of their proponents to accept. Yet, as noted in another recent review of such laws, the facts seem clear enough: "Juvenile curfew laws have been adopted by a great many municipalities in an effort to control juvenile crime; but *no juvenile curfew law has successfully withstood a constitutional challenge in an American appellate court.*"[23]

---

[23] J. Thompson: Police controls over citizen use of the public streets. *The Journal of Criminal Law, Criminology and Police Science,* 49 (March-April, 1959), pp. 562-568.

Although much attention has been given to curfew laws, even more has been given to the charge that our courts are not sufficiently punitive with the parents of delinquents. At one extreme some have demanded a general "get tough" policy. Others have just as strongly deplored such a "negative" approach. The controversy has become categorical, thereby obscuring the subtleties of the issue. You are either "for" or "against" punishment; conversely, you are either "for" or "against" treatment. Again the debate waxeth hot in the absence of clear proof regarding the efficacy of either approach.

The nature of the debate is well illustrated by attempts in New York City to secure adoption of a local law for fining the parents of vandals. In the early 1950's the Park Association of the City of New York and other groups vigorously campaigned for the passage of a law whereby parents and others having custody of juveniles who willfully destroyed city property might be fined up to twenty-five dollars if they failed to exercise reasonable diligence in controlling their children.[24] Such a bill was approved by the City Council but in early 1953 was not passed by the Board of Estimate. On subsequent occasions, the last time in 1959, similar bills were again passed by the City Council and were again killed by the Board of Estimate. The 1953 bill had been supported by a number of civic and religious leaders and by most New York City newspapers. It had been vigorously opposed by child welfare groups, and especially by a majority of the justices of the New York City Domestic Relations Court who, through the Presiding Justice, asserted in letters written to members of the Board of Estimate that:

> The duty of the Children's Court is to treat, rehabilitate, and not punish the child. Treatment of the child requires parental sympathy and cooperation. Punishment of parents creates and widens a breach between parent and child thus impeding treatment, and renders work with the parent all but impossible.[25]

---

[24] For a draft of this law and for statements by individuals supporting its adoption, see *Vandalism in City Parks.* New York, The Park Association of the City of New York, April, 1952.

[25] W. Gellhorn, *et al.: Children and Families in the Courts of New York City.* New York, Dodd, Mead and Company, 1954, p. 71, n. 13.

It is interesting to compare this statement with those made by other juvenile court judges relative to punishing the parents of delinquents. Thus Judge Paul W. Alexander, reputed to run a "one-chance" court where adults are concerned (i.e., a court where an adult gets only one chance to make good on a suspended sentence and if he appears again he goes to prison),[26] evaluated a ten-year policy of punishing parents in Toledo, Ohio, by concluding:

> In fine, we might say our study seems to show that to punish parents who contribute to the delinquency or neglect of their children accomplishes very few, if any of the things claimed for it except revenge; *that in some cases where the parent is refractory and resists the case-work approach, a certain amount of actual punishment may bring about co-operation; that in selected cases, where other methods have failed, prosecution and the threat of punishment, without actual punishment, are rather effective* (italics not in the original).
>
> But punishing parents is no panacea.[27]

George W. Smyth, while judge of the Westchester County Children's Court, New York, took a position similar to that taken by Judge Alexander. He stated that although the persuasive service of the juvenile court "enlists the co-operation of most parents, some always will remain deaf to persuasion. The law, therefore, wisely empowers the court to deal authoritatively with these recalcitrant parents." Cautioning against the use of such

---

[26] P. W. Alexander: What's this about punishing parents? *Federal Probation,* 12 (March, 1948), pp. 23-29.

[27] *Ibid.*

It is interesting to note that this article, perhaps the most quoted reference in the literature about punishing parents, has been used to support both sides in the "punishing parents controversy." Thus, Gellhorn (*op. cit.,* pp. 72-73) and Judge J. W. Polier of the New York City Domestic Relations Court (The woodshed is no answer. *Federal Probation,* 20, September, 1956, pp. 3-5) have used Alexander's comments to support their opposition to punishing parents. On the other hand, the *Report of the New York State Temporary Commission on Youth and Delinquency* (December, 1955, p. 35) interprets the article as urging widespread punishment for the parents of delinquents. The reader is urged to read the reference for himself and draw his own conclusions as to its meaning.

power for the purpose of blind punishment, he added, "I have found that charging the parent with the misdemeanor of contributing where the facts warrant such charge, and upon conviction imposing a stiff fine, is very effective. Well placed publicity concerning the fine stopped an epidemic of automobile stealing."[28]

Is the position taken by the New York justices irreconcilable with that taken by Judges Alexander and Smyth? Perhaps. In any case, there seems to be no conclusive reason why in *selected* cases, where other methods have failed and in full accord with the principles of remedial justice, recalcitrant parents who are willfully contributing to the delinquency, including the vandalism, of their children should not be dealt with authoritatively. Such procedure, applied with discretion and not indiscriminately against the parents of all delinquents, would in no way violate the premise that "neither the procedures nor the traditional attitudes of the criminal courts should find any large part in a court concerned with children."[29] After all, "the most 'moderate' of the experts in the field seem to feel that punishment can play a constructive role in rehabilitation, if it is applied planfully and for helpful rather than vengeful purposes."[30] Although the latter remark was made about the punishment of delinquents, it would seem to apply with equal validity to their parents.

Although this policy might in some ways be facilitated by the enactment of special legislation, such as laws enabling courts to fine the parents of vandals, the application of negative sanctions to culpable parents is scarcely dependent upon new legislation. The application of such sanctions is entirely feasible under the provisions of existing legislation in most jurisdictions. Negative sanctions, for example, may be applied to culpable parents in all but two states (Delaware and Vermont) under statutes which provide for punishing parents who contribute to the neglect or delinquency of their children. Or, in the special case of vandalism, parents who are financially able might be encouraged by

---

[28] G. W. Smyth: The juvenile court and delinquent parents. *Federal Probation,* 13 (March, 1949), pp. 12-17.

[29] Gellhorn, *op. cit.,* p. 74.

[30] H. Epstein: *Perspectives on Delinquency Prevention.* New York, 1955, p. 10.

courts to pay for the damage done by their children as part of the disposition process in such cases, as when restitution is made one of the conditions of probation.

When practices such as these are not followed in courts even in cases where they might reasonably be applied, it is doubtful that inadequate legislation is to blame. It is far more probable that the fault lies with individual judges, who, categorically refusing to use punishment as an acceptable alternative in their courts, refuse to apply negative sanctions to parents under almost any circumstances.

Aside from curfews and the punishing of parents, various kinds of "protective" devices have been implemented or recommended for the prevention of vandalism and other types of delinquency. Two of the most imaginative are illustrated in the following news reports. The first describes a device for protecting schools from vandals in Hackensack, New Jersey. The second refers to a technique proposed in New York City for protecting parks from vandals and other undesirables.

School Vandals Curbed by Hidden Microphones

HACKENSACK, N. J., March 19—Hidden microphones have been installed in this city's seven schools to prevent vandalism. The microphones are connected with police headquarters by leased telephone lines.

The system is turned on when the schools are closed. If the sound level rises above the normal quiet in any building, an alarm goes off at headquarters and a red light designates the school.

The system was installed by the Board of Education about six weeks ago at a cost of $10,000. In a long series of vandalism in the schools, a fire set in one building last spring caused damages of $80,000.

No attempts at vandalism have been made since the microphones were set up, George A. Brown, president of the Board of Education said today.[31]

---

[31] *The New York Times,* March 20, 1958.

PARK UNIT CONSIDERS USING
DOG PATROLS TO FLUSH VANDALS

A proposal for using dog patrols to rid the city's parks of vandals and other undesirables is being studied by the Park Association of New York City.

Charles G. Meyer, president of the association, disclosed yesterday that the proposal envisions the financing of the patrols by the association. He explained that his organization would have to increase greatly its present membership of about 300, and that the purchase and upkeep of the dogs would be financed with the help of the additional dues. The Police Department, he said, has begun a study of the possible use of such patrols. . . .

Mr. Meyer told the group that there was need for more policing of the parks but that more policemen were not available. He said that in London Labrador retrievers were used in patrolling the parks. These dogs, he declared, were tame and lovable and were used "to get into the bushes and flush out undesirable characters."[32]

Another interesting development is the "vandal squad" in Los Angeles described in the following report.

VANDAL SQUAD

The vandals who broke into the Malabar School on Los Angeles' overcrowded east side did a thoroughgoing job. They whirled through nine classrooms, the athletic rooms, the teachers' kitchen and dining room. They broke chairs and tables, splattered ink over the walls, smashed whatever clocks they happened to find. Last week the five boys responsible found out that crime doesn't pay. It had taken L. A.'s special school security section only a few hours to track them down.

In its six years, the security section has chalked up a record that any large city might envy. When former School Superintendent Alexander Stoddard set it up in 1948, Los Angeles was suffering a postwar boom in delinquency. Last week—in spite of the fact that the juvenile crime rate throughout the rest of the city has climbed 16%—the school system announced that

[32] *Ibid.*, June 19, 1957.

its annual bill for burglary and vandalism has been cut from $300,000 to $127,000.

From his cluttered office in the headquarters of the board of education, Section Chief Robert O. Graham, 49, runs his 33 agents, watchmen and clerks like a miniature FBI. His twelve special agents have all served on police forces, must take courses in law and psychology before earning their deputy's badge from the sheriff. Though they turn some cases (e.g., truancy and dope peddling) over to other authorities, their own quarry includes every one from the little boy who steals ice cream to the crackpot who might threaten to shoot the superintendent.

Last year all but 25 of the city's 500 schools were forced to call on Graham's agents. There were 25 cases of arson, 342 of vandalism, 182 of theft, 947 of burglary, 37 involving such miscellaneous matters as damage to a school lawn. But Graham's cases are steadily dwindling. The number of arrests last week: 24. The weekly average a year ago: 50.[33]

No effort will be made to evaluate precisely the efficacy of alarm systems, patrol dogs, or special vandal squads. However, although techniques of this kind do little to modify the basic attitudes and values of vandals, or to alleviate the social and cultural conditions giving rise to vandalism, all such devices can be used to give increased police protection to schools and other buildings and areas. The difficulty, of course, is that boys may soon learn to circumvent such stratagems or, as seems more likely and in keeping with their versatility, to direct their vexing talents elsewhere.

Turning now to perhaps more sagacious proposals that have been made for preventing delinquency, we find "that those concerned with prevention define it in one of three ways: (1) the sum total of all activities that contribute to the adjustment of children and to healthy personalities in children; (2) attempts to deal with particular environmental conditions that are believed to contribute to delinquency; and (3) specific preventive services provided to individual or groups of children."[34]

---

[33] *Time,* 64 (November 8, 1954), p. 90.

[34] H. A. Bloch and F. T. Flynn: *Delinquency: The Juvenile Offender in America Today.* New York: Random House, 1956, p. 512.

The logic underlying preventive activities of the first type is disarmingly simple: anything that contributes to the adjustment of children and to their healthy personality development prevents delinquency. Basically this approach links delinquency prevention with general improvements in the institutional fabric of our society, particularly as these affect child welfare. In large part this approach rests on a continuation and extension of measures, now commonplace on the American scene, which are designed to reduce the economic inequities of our social system. Such activities include procedures for raising the income levels of poverty-stricken families, better low-rent housing, improving job tenure and work arrangements, and other means for reducing the rigors of poverty and economic insecurity. The approach also embraces attempts to reduce prejudice and discrimination against minority group people, increase the educational achievements of oncoming generations, improve marital relations by premarital counseling and family social work, as well as efforts to increase the impact of religious doctrines upon both adults and children in our communities.

Preventive activities of the second type, by and large, aim to overcome factors in the immediate environment of children that seem to contribute to their delinquency. Such activities include attempts at community organization, such as the Chicago Area Projects to be discussed later in this chapter, "co-ordinating councils" that try better to co-ordinate the efforts of welfare and child care agencies in delinquency prevention, recreational and character-building agencies of all types, as well as attempts to reduce the commercial activities of adults which are clearly illegal and detrimental to the welfare of children who may get caught up in such traffic, as for example, the sale of liquor to minors, dope peddling, and the reception of stolen goods.

Preventive activities of the third type include probation and parole services to children and youths, the programs of residential institutions and special schools for delinquents, child guidance clinics, insofar as they are concerned with the diagnosis and treatment of delinquents, direct work with antisocial street gangs, and a variety of other services whose principal purpose is the adjustment of individual children or groups of children.

It would be enormously difficult, if not impossible, to measure the effectiveness of these three types of preventive activities in terms of their ability actually to reduce delinquency, and no attempt will be made to do so here.[35] However, general comment will be made about the relative merits of the three approaches.

In the main it is perhaps correct to conclude that improvement in the collective welfare, particularly in the welfare of depressed minority people, will reduce delinquency. The fact is that in areas such as metropolitan New York, the reduction of juvenile delinquency appears to be most intimately linked with the successful assimilation of low-status groups, in particular the ever increasing number of migrant and uprooted Negroes and Puerto Ricans living in such communities.[36] Whatever contributes to the welfare and assimilation of these people reduces delinquency rates among their children and, correspondingly in the communities in which they live. Conversely, whatever impedes their progress inflates delinquency rates in their areas of residence.

Nevertheless the relationship between delinquency and improvement in the general welfare seems to be more complicated than it appears at first glance. For example, although it is tempting to claim that improved housing and the reduction of poverty will reduce both crime and delinquency, evidence that delinquency is highest during periods of extreme prosperity and *not* during depressions,[37] as well as awareness of the variety and number of offenses committed by middle and upper-class people should warn us against the facile assumption that the elimination of poverty is the Rosetta stone of crime prevention.

The relationship between delinquency, at least in terms of official statistics, and poverty and poor housing has, of course,

---

[35] For an excellent discussion of the problems involved in evaluating delinquency prevention programs, as well as for a review of the attempts that have been made to evaluate particular programs, see H. L. Witmer and E. Tufts: *The Effectiveness of Delinquency Prevention Programs.* Children's Bureau, United States Department of Health, Education, and Welfare, Publication 350. Washington, Government Printing Office, 1954.

[36] For an excellent discussion of this point, see O. Handlin: *The Newcomers.* Cambridge, Massachusetts, Harvard University Press, 1959, especially chap. 4.

[37] See P. W. Tappan: *Juvenile Delinquency.* New York, McGraw-Hill Book Company, 1949, pp. 142-145.

long been noted by students of social problems.[38] However, it seems erroneous to conclude from this that the abolishment of these living conditions will also abolish delinquency among low-status children for, as Bernard Lander demonstrated in his study of differential juvenile delinquency rates by census tracts in Baltimore,[39] delinquency appears to be fundamentally related to social instability or *anomie* and not basically to poverty and poor housing. Thus, as he concluded in part:

> The delinquency rate is fundamentally related only to the *anomie* and not specifically to the socio-economic conditions of an area. The delinquency rate in a *stable* community will be low in spite of its being characterized by bad housing, poverty and propinquity to the city center. On the other hand, one would expect a high delinquency rate in an area characterized by normlessness and social instability. In such sections there is a deficiency in the traditional social controls which maintain conventional behavior in stable communities.[40]

It is within this context that the disillusionment of those who expected too much by way of delinquency prevention from public housing can best be understood. Their disappointment is well reflected in the pungent remark reportedly made by one student of New York's slums: "Once upon a time we thought that if we could only get our problem families out of those dreadful slums, then papa would stop taking dope, mama would stop chasing around, and Junior would stop carrying a knife. Well, we've got them in a nice apartment with modern kitchens and a recreation center. And they're the same bunch of bastards they always were."[41]

Emphasis upon *anomie* or social disorganization as a basic contributing factor to the high delinquency rates characteristic of

---

[38] See, e.g., C. R. Shaw and H. D. McKay: *Juvenile Delinquency and Urban Areas.* Chicago, University of Chicago Press, 1942.

[39] B. Lander: *Towards an Understanding of Juvenile Delinquency.* New York, Columbia University Press, 1954.

[40] *Ibid.,* p. 89. (Reprinted by permission.)

[41] D. Seligman: The enduring slums, in The Editors of Fortune, *The Exploding Metropolis.* Garden City, New York, Doubleday and Company, 1958, pp. 111-132.

some urban areas, with a concomitant de-emphasis upon the obvious poverty of these areas as the underlying factor in their high delinquency rates, would, then, appear to be of cardinal importance for understanding and preventing delinquency in such areas.

Useful as Lander's statistical analysis of census tracts in Baltimore may be for destroying the myth that poverty and inadequate housing are the root causes of delinquency, the relationship between *anomie* and delinquency may also be more complicated than it seems. Lander emphasized the "internal" disorganization characteristic of high delinquency areas. Yet relatively *stable* neighborhoods may also be characterized by comparatively high rates of delinquency. A good example of just such a neighborhood is the tightly-knit Italian slum of "Eastern City" examined by William Foote Whyte in his classic, *Street Corner Society.*[42]

The existence of stable but delinquent neighborhoods suggests that there are at least two kinds of delinquency-producing areas. First, there are rapidly changing and thoroughly chaotic local areas of the kind isolated by Lander. Areas of this type are perhaps best illustrated by New York City's racially-mixed and tension-ridden Spanish Harlem so well described by Dan Wakefield in *Island in the City.*[43] Second, there are rather well organized neighborhoods such as the Italian ethnic community studied by Whyte which are "disorganized" primarily in the sense that the way of life in such areas is judged "out of step" when contrasted with the essentially middle-class culture of the greater society.[44]

It is in the second kind of area particularly that well developed relationships are likely to exist between criminally precocious adolescents, corrupt politicians, and the seemingly inevitable racketeers. These relationships go far in explaining the easy transition many delinquents make from juvenile misbehavior to

[42] W. F. Whyte: *Street Corner Society,* enlarged edition. Chicago, University of Chicago Press, 1955.

[43] D. Wakefield: *Island in the City.* Boston, Houghton Mifflin Company, 1959.

[44] For a further discussion of these two kinds of delinquency areas, see W. F. Whyte: Social organization in the slums. *American Sociological Review,* 8 (February, 1943), pp. 34-39.

the more sophisticated forms of adult criminality. It is in this type of area, too, that personality and family structures are less likely to split and disintegrate under the stresses and strains characteristic of more chaotic and tension-ridden neighborhoods.

But distinctions of this sort, important as they may be for understanding differences in the social structure of delinquency areas, must not obscure a more basic fact: quite aside from the stability or instability of social relations in delinquency-prone areas the traditions, standards, and moral sentiments of such areas are notoriously delinquent and criminal in "complexion" and "tone." This peculiar cultural climate has long been recognized by students of urban life, particularly by the ecologists and social psychologists of the "Chicago School" in American sociology.[45]

In more recent years, this recognition has been linked up with a more general discussion of social class subcultures and particularly with more detailed analyses of lower-class culture as a breeding ground for delinquency. A good example of this is found in a recent article by Walter B. Miller which called attention to the delinquency-proneness of lower-class culture in a discussion of the "focal concerns" of the urban lower-class way of life.[46] Miller's emphasis is not upon the so-called "subculture of the delinquent gang" as discussed by Cohen, but upon the content of the whole mode of existence of urban lower-class people. Miller believes that in the lower-class, in contrast with the middle-class, people are likely to have commitments to focal concerns such as physical "toughness," "smartness" interpreted as the ability to "con" or dupe others, and "excitement" in terms of seeking thrills, taking risks, and courting danger. When these commitments are combined with the intense need for "in-group" membership and status or "rep" so characteristic of lower-class adolescents, Miller feels that conditions are especially ripe for the development of juvenile misconduct, especially gang delinquency.

---

[45] For an excellent survey of studies in the "social ecology" of crime conducted during the past 150 years, see T. Morris: *The Criminal Area.* London, Routledge and Kegan Paul, 1958, chaps. I-VI.

[46] W. B. Miller: Lower class culture as a generating milieu of gang delinquency. *The Journal of Social Issues, 41:*3 (1958), pp. 5-19.

Thus the concept of social disorganization can be used to describe both stable and unstable delinquency areas. If we accept such disorganization as basic to an understanding of law violation in both kinds of areas, then we must question the value of other delinquency prevention methods besides those aimed at the reduction of poverty. In particular we should examine the limitations inherent in current attempts to prevent delinquency by the use of "individual-centered" techniques, such as social case work and related psychological-psychiatric services.

Practitioners of such techniques work toward individual adjustment, not social change. Seldom do they try to reduce the delinquency-producing features of the delinquent's environment, especially his extra-familial environment; instead they emphasize adjustment to prevailing environmental conditions. For most delinquents, in the last analysis, this means that they are expected to make a non-delinquent adjustment to a highly delinquent life situation. Our recidivism rates testify that at best this adjustment is precarious. Furthermore, and this is perhaps the more basic point, because such efforts fail to come to grips with the underlying social and cultural conditions giving rise to delinquency, they do little to prevent the outcropping of delinquency in the first instance. Most try to take hold only after maladjustment, even delinquency itself, has become manifest in the lives of the youngsters they seek to help.

This, however, should not be taken as a rejection of probation and parole, of training schools and reformatories, of child guidance clinics, and of other kinds of institutions and agencies given over to the care and "correction" of delinquents. Far from abandoning this line of approach, we must work hard at improving existing facilities of this sort and act imaginatively regarding the "invention" of new ones. Furthermore, we must, as we have seldom paused to do in the past, rigorously test and verify the effectiveness of various approaches aimed at the rehabilitation of individual delinquents. In this regard the basic question still to be answered is: To what extent and under what conditions do our correctional agencies really correct?

But despite all of this, we must not be so carried away by our desire to rehabilitate delinquents that we fail to see individual treatment in a proper perspective, lose sight of its limitations, and ignore the fundamental proposition that *the prevention of delinquency should include both individual treatment and general or social prevention.* Unfortunately this is just what has happened. To a truly remarkable degree public and private delinquency prevention agencies have spent comparatively little money or energy on community-centered programs of social prevention. For decades most of these agencies have put their effort into establishing various kinds of facilities for rehabilitating delinquents on a case-by-case basis with the "model" and most prestigeful approach in recent years being that of the psychiatrically-oriented child guidance clinic.

In sum, granting the primary role social disorganization plays in the development of delinquency, then the prevention of delinquency is not fundamentally a problem of bettering the general welfare of children or rehabilitating individuals, although the wisdom of continuing our attempts at both seems obvious. Nor for that matter is delinquency prevention essentially a problem of co-ordinating the activity of welfare agencies, although, like the application of "individual-centered" techniques, this too has an important role to play in prevention. The co-ordination of agency activity is particularly valuable insofar as it enables accurate statistics on reported delinquency to be gathered in various jurisdictions, for it is only on the basis of such statistics that a community can determine the trend of its delinquency and measure the effectiveness of its preventive efforts. Agency co-ordination is even more valuable when it serves to bring various preventive programs and techniques to bear on potential delinquents before their deviancy becomes well established.

Basically, however, the problem of delinquency prevention is a problem of social organization or reorganization and other approaches have merit only to the degree that they contribute to such reorganization.

How can social reorganization best be accomplished? Although we may be both unable and unwilling to reduce substantially the drift toward *anomie* that Merton has suggested is a pervasive characteristic of our society,[47] we may be able to make partial

[47] Merton, *Social Theory and Social Structure, op. cit.*, chap. IV.

inroads upon such disorganization, particularly insofar as it is related to the problems of juvenile delinquency, if we focus directly on the local areas in which delinquency is most pronounced. The logic underlying this proposal is that a local area "does not need to control the entire culture of a nation (which would be impossible) in order to control its delinquency rate. The things that need to be done are local and relate to personal interaction rather than to the larger institutions."[48] The essence of this approach to social reorganization, then, is to stimulate social change in delinquency-prone neighborhoods.

Unfortunately we have no rich arsenal of tried and proven techniques for accomplishing this change. Much needs to be learned and many innovations need to be developed toward this end. Despite these difficulties, however, we do know much about stimulating change in delinquency areas. The framework within which the reorganization of such neighborhoods can be accomplished has been well described by Thrasher in his outline of a proposal for co-ordinating neighborhood activity for delinquency prevention.[49]

This proposal envisions that any attempt to prevent delinquency in local areas must fix responsibility for social change at the neighborhood level where such change can be implemented by local community leaders assisted by experts. Implicit in this approach is the assumption that in even the most delinquency-prone neighborhoods not all the residents are criminals or delinquents, and that in such areas there is actually a duality of conduct norms—one favoring law-abiding behavior, the other favoring delinquency.[50]

Although as subsidiary techniques Thrasher's plan utilizes the best services offered by the usual community agencies, especially those of school, court, training institutions, and child guidance

---

[48] E. H. Sutherland: Prevention of juvenile delinquency, in Cohen, *et al., op. cit.*, pp. 131-140.

[49] F. M. Thrasher: Some principles underlying community co-ordination. *The Journal of Educational Sociology,* 18 (March, 1945), pp. 387-400.

[50] For a discussion of the duality of conduct norms in delinquency areas, see S. Korbin: The conflict of values in delinquency areas. *American Sociological Review,* 16 (October, 1951), pp. 653-661.

clinic, it must be emphasized that his proposal "represents a radical departure from the methods of social work and community organization as formerly conceived."[51]

This comment made almost three decades ago is nearly as applicable now as it was then. When one surveys current social work efforts at community organization, it becomes abundantly clear that, far from being focused on local areas, this activity is largely county or city-wide in scope. Furthermore, all too often "community organization" in social work means that professional social workers meet with each other and with upper and middle-class laymen for the purposes of mapping fund-raising campaigns, educating the public, co-ordinating agency activity, and similar objectives. Even when particular neighborhoods are the targets for such organization, seldom is the basic responsibility for such work placed in the hands of leaders who, in terms of their social class, ethnic, and religious affiliations, are truly representative of the people living in such areas.

Fundamentally the difference between the kind of plan outlined by Thrasher and traditional social work proposals for community organization is that in the former the real work is done by local residents who, banded together in a committee or council, act to: (1) get the facts about delinquents and delinquency in their neighborhood; (2) organize existing preventive forces serving their neighborhood; (3) stimulate the development of new programs and services as required; and (4) in co-operation with professional agencies, look to the adjustment of their own delinquents, organize the leisure-time activities of their own children and young people, and improve the neighborhood environment, particularly by encouraging the enforcement of laws outlawing the activities of "slum landlords," petty racketeers, and other adults that are clearly detrimental to the welfare of their neighborhood and their children.

Other sociologists besides Thrasher have also foreseen the urgency of organizing the local community for delinquency prevention. Thus Sutherland, for example, endorsed local community

---

[51] F. M. Thrasher: *The Gang*, second revised edition. Chicago, University of Chicago Press, 1936, p. 538.

organization as the most effective means for preventing delinquency, emphasized the need for placing responsibility for such organization directly in the hands of those whose children are the most likely to become delinquent, and cited the necessity of including juveniles themselves as participants in such organization.[52]

The inclusion of children and youths in the neighborhood organizations for delinquency prevention is most vital. Too often they are simply "left out" of the planning and management phases of such activity. As a result, the isolation of their adolescence is compounded and a real opportunity for establishing closer ties between the generations is overlooked.

Perhaps the best known of the relatively few delinquency prevention programs predicated on local community organization that are actually in operation are the Chicago Area Projects:

> The area project approach, developed by Clifford R. Shaw and his associates, has been one of the most interesting developments of the past quarter-century. The projects, of which there are now ten in Chicago, attempt to develop a sense of neighborliness and mutual responsibility in specific slum communities. Certain premises underlie this method. In the first place, a central theme of the area project movement is that leadership must be developed within the community and not superimposed from without. Shaw has been extremely critical of the leadership techniques used by a great many traditional agencies, including settlement houses, boys' clubs, and the like, on the grounds that they involve the imposition of leadership and program ideologies from outside the community. In other words, Shaw's point is that somebody else decides what is good for the community, and that this must be replaced by the development of indigenous leadership.
>
> A second concept is that the delinquency-breeding communities can help themselves by the development of an internal cohesiveness based upon activities rooted in concern about delinquency by natural community leaders. This means that through these natural leaders, who may be precinct captains, bartenders, truck-drivers, or local "self-made" businessmen,

[52] Sutherland: Prevention of juvenile delinquency, *op. cit.*

> community deterioration can be halted by involving a substantial number of people who live in slum areas in the kinds of activities that will improve community life and give children an opportunity to grow up in decent and wholesome surroundings.
>
> In the Chicago area projects, the program, which is tailored to meet each community's needs, is centered in a recreational and educational facility. Paramount is the notion that the activities are not an end in themselves but a means of developing unity within the community itself. It is believed that the children drawn into various activities are susceptible to identification with the more conventional forms of American behavior, and that delinquency is largely social in nature, although not exclusively so. Delinquency is considered to be a reaction to a conflict of values in which children are exposed to widely diverse points of view, resulting in confusion and the failure to incorporate acceptable standards of any kind.
>
> The area projects operate through various kinds of neighborhood and community committees which conduct a wide variety of activities, and in addition do some direct work with children of the counseling or person-to-person type. Again, the keynote is that only the person who has status in the community, even a former delinquent, is likely to have influence upon youngsters who live in such communities. Consequently, the use of outside leadership is minimal—chiefly to discover and develop local talent rather than to bring professional resources to bear upon the situation; although in certain instances, apparently relatively few in number, referral to psychiatric resources is made for the youngsters who seem to have underlying personality disturbances.[53]

Thus, although outside leaders have a definite but limited role to play in this approach to area reorganization, principal emphasis is placed on the role of natural community leaders who are carriers of conventional conduct norms. Not only do such leaders serve as non-delinquent models for emulation by youngsters attracted to programs offered by projects of this type, but be-

---

[53] Bloch and Flynn, *op. cit.*, pp. 522-523. (Reprinted by permission.)

For a more detailed description of the Chicago Area Projects, see A. Sorrentino: The Chicago Area Project after 25 years. *Federal Probation*, 23 (June, 1959), pp. 40-45.

cause these indigenous leaders have prestige in the local area, they easily attract adults, as well as children and youths, to project programs in the first instance. It is around natural community leaders, then, that legitimate social structures can be germinated and multiplied in delinquency-prone areas. And it is in relationship with such leaders and within such structures that youngsters can develop the close and intimate attachments with conventional models, achieve the satisfactions, and acquire the sense of personal worth and purpose necessary to counter the drift toward delinquency characteristic of their life situations.

Two basic questions arise relative to preventive programs like the Chicago Area Projects: First, can they be established, and once established will they last? Second, do they actually prevent delinquency?

In regard to the first question, the answer to both points seems to be definitely affirmative. Thus, in their recent evaluation of the Chicago Area Projects, Witmer and Tufts found that:

> 1. Residents of low income areas can and have organized themselves into effective working units for promoting and conducting welfare programs.
> 2. These community organizations have been stable and enduring. They raise funds, administer them well, and adapt the programs to local needs.
> 3. Local talent, otherwise untapped, has been discovered and utilized. Local leadership has been mobilized in the interest of children's welfare.[54]

A definite answer to the second question is much more difficult to obtain. However, two types of evidence tentatively suggest that it too may be affirmative. First, delinquency statistics from 1930 to 1942 indicate that delinquency rates declined in three out of four of the communities in which projects were then being carried on; second, in some of the projects, work with men and boys on parole from institutions has been very successful, with one project noting that out of forty-one parolees worked with between 1935 and 1944, only one was recommitted to an institu-

---

[54] Witmer and Tufts, *op. cit.*, p. 15.

tion.[55] However, evidence such as this, without comparable controls, must obviously remain inconclusive. As has been remarked elsewhere, "the role of any preventive agency is likely to be most difficult to assess."[56] The Chicago Area Projects are no exception.

Another question that arises with respect to delinquency prevention programs geared to local leadership is: How can they best be originated? In this regard Walter C. Reckless has warned against waiting for the "spontaneous generation of experimental action"; outside help must get such programs started by stimulating local leaders to action.[57] Likewise it seems necessary that outside assistance should also include sufficient money, at least in the beginning, to help defray the cost of running such programs. Again and again programs of this type have foundered because the few hundred dollars raised by raffles, cake sales, thrift shops, and local donations were simply not enough to meet day-to-day expenses.

Who should provide such assistance? To this there are a number of answers. The potential role of private foundations, boards of education, fraternal organizations, and private industry and labor unions in supporting or initiating such activity is enormous. Of special significance is the potential but presently underdeveloped role urban churches can play in this field. The force of organized religion in the prevention of delinquency will be more fully realized if, and only if, more churches make realistic financial appropriations for such purpose and if, on the personal level, more churchmen base their approach to delinquents on love, direct service, intimate communication, and example, instead of on benign indifference, social distance, and exhortation.[58]

---

[55] *Ibid.*, p. 16.

[56] Bloch and Flynn, *op. cit.*, p. 514.

[57] W. C. Reckless: *The Crime Problem.* New York, Appleton-Century-Crofts, 1950, pp. 524-525.

[58] For excellent descriptions of religious programs in which churchmen have established intimate relationships with gang members and other residents of delinquency-prone neighborhoods, see C. K. Myers: *Light the Dark Streets.* Greenwich, Connecticut, Seabury Press, 1957, and H. J. Rahm and J. R. Weber: *Office in the Alley: Report on a Project with Gang Youngsters.* University of Texas, Austin, Hogg Foundation for Mental Health, 1958.

Assistance should also be available from other sources. For example, communities in states with Youth Authority Plans[59] might well call upon such authorities for help insofar as these state agencies actually make provision for realistic assistance to local communities; and in New York the new State Youth Division, one purpose of which is to stimulate communities to take action with regard to delinquency, should be a prime source of both money and advice, as should the Youth Board in New York City. Although the Federal Youth Corrections Act[60] makes no provision for rendering assistance to local communities, the capacity of the Federal Government in this and other facets of community programs for delinquency prevention is tremendous. Finally, professional social workers themselves, as citizens, as agency representatives and educators, and as spokesmen for their highly influential professional associations, might become less remiss about endorsing, inaugurating, and experimenting with community-centered crime prevention programs.

In any event, if neighborhood programs run by residents are to develop to their full potential, it seems almost axiomatic that outside assistance must be provided.

RECOMMENDATIONS FOR THE PREVENTION OF VANDALISM

Society's most immediate defense against the criminal and the delinquent is the police. Backed by the courts and various "correctional" agencies which deal with offenders on a case-by-case basis, the police remain indispensable in the prevention of crime and delinquency. Yet these problems are rooted in such a variety of personal pathologies and social-cultural dislocations that no community troubled by law violation can afford to depend simply upon its police, courts, and public and private agencies which are concerned with the care and adjustment of individual offend-

[59] By the end of 1953, eight states (California, Minnesota, Wisconsin, Massachusetts, Texas, Arizona, Kentucky, and Illinois) and the Federal Government had enacted some type of youth authority legislation. Bloch and Flynn, *op. cit.*, p. 487.

[60] For a description of the provisions of the Federal Youth Corrections Act which is entirely oriented toward the treatment of youthful offenders convicted in federal courts, see G. J. Reed: The Federal Youth Corrections Act. *Federal Probation,* 18 (September, 1954), pp. 10-15.

ers. More must be done than can possibly be accomplished by these agencies of social control.

The truth of this proposition is clearly evident in the material presented in the preceding pages of this study. The prevention of vandalism and other types of delinquency must involve both good law-enforcement and good individual treatment and custodial care. But more importantly, it must also involve community-centered approaches to delinquency prevention.

Of the three types of vandals described in Chapter III, those classified as Essentially Law-Abiding are obviously the ones most likely to respond favorably to almost any preventive effort. Boys of this type, without serious personal and/or social pathologies, are the so-called "easy cases" with which agencies engaged in delinquency prevention must deal. In fact, some youngsters of this type may actually require little or no care or assistance. When they do need help, perhaps the most obvious and direct approach is through the use of "specific preventive services," such as counseling, case work, and when necessary, psychiatry.

Unfortunately only a minority of vandals appear to be boys of this type. Of the others, some appear to fall into the category of Disturbed Vandals, but most seem best classified as Subcultural Vandals. The former are characterized by serious personality disturbances, while the latter are distinguished by their exposure to and participation in the delinquent subculture.

This leads to the conclusion that while case work and family counseling, psychiatry, various group psychotherapies, and related "individual-centered" techniques may be applied with considerable success to Essentially Law-Abiding Vandals, the use of such techniques with Disturbed and Subcultural Vandals will probably meet with only limited success. In fact, once the personality systems of youngsters become grossly disorganized, as in the case of Disturbed Vandals, rehabilitation by any known techniques, or combination of techniques, becomes extremely doubtful. When such boys become dangerous to themselves and to the community, the only real alternative is commitment to a state hospital or similar facility.

The problem with Subcultural Vandals is considerably different. Here if a particular boy's behavior becomes overly aggressive and dangerous, commitment not to a state hospital but to a correctional institution may be required. But this is only an interim device which may or may not lead to his rehabilitation, and may or may not provide the community with an opportunity to "win over" the gang of which he is perhaps a significant and influential member. Accepting the thesis that the vandalism and other delinquency committed by such boys occurs largely as a consequence of the delinquency proneness characteristic of their neighborhoods of residence, the essential problem is to do something about the features of the local areas in which Subcultural Vandals have been reared and to which they will return after leaving a correctional institution.

Thus, although many Subcultural Vandals need the support of case workers, psychiatrists, and other interested persons, the "rehabilitation" of such boys is not basically a problem of rehabilitating *individuals.* It is, instead a problem of altering the immediate and delinquency-prone environment in which such boys live and to which they respond.

Case material in Chapter III describes the delinquency-producing qualities of the local areas in which Disturbed Vandals live. More significantly the material also draws attention to the rootless and isolated nature of the life situations of such boys. Thus, insofar as the personal pathologies and the delinquency of Disturbed Vandals arise out of the features of their life circumstances, the reduction of local *anomie* may also prove useful in minimizing the development of gross personality disturbances and delinquency among youngsters of this type.

Put simply, unlike the prevention of vandalism by Essentially Law-Abiding Vandals, the prevention of vandalism and other types of delinquency by Subcultural and Disturbed Vandals is largely a problem of social reorganization on the neighborhood level. The best method for effecting such reorganization is, as has previously been proposed, to encourage residents of disorganized neighborhoods to band together in committees or councils and to look after the adjustment of their own children and the welfare of their own neighborhoods.

It is in terms of this orientation that the other characteristics of vandals and vandalism described in Chapter II have utility as guides to prevention. Thus, taking cognizance of the age, sex, and ethnic characteristics of vandals, and the type of residential areas in which they are concentrated, programs especially interested in preventing vandalism should single out for particular attention younger, white boys living in delinquency-prone neighborhoods. In addition, because vandalism seems to be almost always a group offense, such programs should focus particularly on groups of boys found in such areas.

One of the underlying assumptions of the present study was that vandalism, as a type of human behavior, is not aimless activity but is directed toward the achievement of some end or goal. Moreover, vandalism as goal-directed behavior occurs only under conditions called "situations."

The purposes of vandalism and the various "situations of conflict" in which it finds expression were described in Chapter IV. It is evident from this material that, besides focusing on particular kinds of youngsters, their families, peer groups, and neighborhoods, programs for preventing vandalism should also vigilantly guard against particular "situations" especially likely to "trigger off" such delinquent acts.

Thus, for example, in communities characterized by latent racial tensions care might be taken to anticipate, to contain, and to resolve as deftly as possible particular crises as they may develop between racial groups. Of course the underlying prejudices and antagonisms out of which such crises emerge will not be directly reduced by the maintenance of public order through police vigilance or by the resolution of immediate issues through compromise. Long established feelings separating racial groups do not promptly evaporate just because on-the-spot conflicts are resolved; the elimination of such deep-seated cleavages requires much more sweeping social change. But the rapid and successful containment or elimination of immediate "occasions of strain" may be expected to accomplish at least two things. First, in the absence of such strain intergroup tensions will be reduced and, concomitantly, there will be less likelihood that vandalism and other types of violence will be directed across racial lines, especially by adolescents and youths who are quick to respond to such tensions and to engage in such disorders. Second, resolving immediate sources of strain may well provide a basis for future intergroup communication and accommodation.

In the same manner attention might also be given to arresting the development of tension and conflict between adults who own or control property and the juveniles with whom they come in contact. Teachers, librarians, shopkeepers, home owners, and others who enter into conflict with the types of boys described in this study seem to run special risks of becoming the victims of vandalism. The task, therefore, is to avoid wherever possible instances of such conflict.

The avoidance of conflict between boys and others in their operating milieu may be expected not only to reduce the incidence of situations to which boys are likely to respond by committing acts of vandalism, but may also serve to reduce vandalism and other types of delinquency in a more long-term sense. Thrasher has described the crucial role played by conflict in the development and integration of well-knit delinquent gangs.[61] Play-groups and neighborhood cliques become gangs when they begin to excite disapproval and opposition, develop a definite group consciousness, and become conflict groups.[62] Therefore, to the extent that conflict between groups of boys and others can be reduced, the development of gangs may be forestalled and, in turn, the occurrence of the vandalism and other bizarre delinquency committed by such groups may be decreased.

The "situational" appoach to vandalism prevention might also be practiced with some promise of success in areas where vandalism of the "junking" variety is a problem. Here, through the use of police power and other devices, particular attention might be given to discouraging junk men from buying obviously stolen scrap metal and other material from youngsters. If the sale of such items were no longer feasible, boys might be less inclined to destroy property in order to obtain scrap to sell as junk.

The same kind of approach might also prove helpful in preventing vandalism of the type committed by children who damage property in the course of their play and exploration. The

---

61 Thrasher, *op. cit.*, chaps. II and III.

62 *Ibid.*, p. 30.

ability of planned recreation to prevent delinquency has no doubt been exaggerated. In spite of this, supervised recreation of a kind that will excite and hold the interest of potentially delinquent youngsters may well perform a useful role in preventing "playful" vandalism and similar kinds of petty delinquency. Quite aside from any influence it may or may not have on their subsequent delinquent careers, participation in supervised recreation increases the circle of control the community has over such youngsters and gives them that much less free time to roam the streets of their neighborhoods in search of "fun" and excitement.

Clearly not all "situations" likely to set off vandalism by juveniles can be accurately identified, described, and anticipated. Certainly not all of them can be avoided. Nevertheless, in combination with other approaches to delinquency prevention, the "situational" approach may also prove useful in reducing the incidence of vandalism.

Individuals and groups interested in vandalism might use the conclusions presented in this study as "bench marks" to direct their own investigations and to guide their efforts to prevent such property destruction. It must be emphasized, however, that these conclusions are highly tentative. Obviously we have much to learn about vandalism and its prevention. Toward this end the basic hypotheses and conceptualizations developed in this study need to be tested rigorously again and again under different conditions in various kinds of communities, large and small. It is hoped that this book will encourage such research.

INDEX

D

E

F

G

H

I